DEMON IN MY VIEW

DEMON
IN MY VIEW

by
Arthur Henley

TRIDENT PRESS, NEW YORK
1966

I am grateful to many people for their help in making this book possible. The names of some appear in these pages; the names of many others do not, nor is it possible to list them all.

In a general way, these must include the members of the Montanari staff; professional people, civic leaders, and public officials of the city of Hialeah; and Monty's former classmates and teachers at Winchendon, Massachusetts, at Antioch College, and at Western Carolina College.

I am especially grateful to Dr. Robert L. Wolk, psychologist, of New York City, for reading the manuscript and making valuable suggestions.

My particular thanks go to Monty himself who allowed me to encroach upon his time, pick his brains, and range freely about his facilities to collect this material.

Finally, I am indebted to the children mentioned here, and to their parents and parent-substitutes, for their magnificent cooperation in this endeavor.

But these acknowledgments would not be complete without mention of my wife, Janet, who gave me invaluable assistance in researching the case material and who shared with me both the joy and the burden that accompanied this task.

The children in this book are real. Names and other means of identification have been changed in order that their place in society may not be jeopardized further.

One chapter was published, in somewhat different form, in the *Saturday Evening Post*.

A. H.

To every child's dearest friend and worst enemy—
who all too often is one and the same person.

From childhood's hour I have not been
As others were; I have not seen
As others saw; I could not bring
My passions from a common spring.
From the same source I have not taken
My sorrow; I could not awaken
My heart to joy at the same tone;
And all I loved, I loved alone.
Then—in my childhood, in the dawn
Of a most stormy life—was drawn
From every depth of good and ill
The mystery which binds me still;
From the torrent or the fountain,
From the red cliff of the mountain,
From the sun that round me rolled
In its autumn tint of gold,
From the lightning in the sky
As it passed me flying by,
From the thunder and the storm,
And the cloud that took the form
(When the rest of Heaven was blue)
Of a demon in my view.

—EDGAR ALLAN POE

I

A JETLINER FROM LOS ANGELES touched down at Miami Airport on an April afternoon and swung open its doors to reveal a shocking sight. A scrawny little girl, straining at a leash held by her mother, came scrambling down the ramp like a dog. Her hands were upraised, the fingers curled into the palms. She walked with the loping gait of a dog on its hind legs, bared her teeth in a menacing growl, and snapped and snarled at the astonished crowd.

"Oh, it's just a stunt," one spectator scoffed. "The kid is probably in some new movie."

"My God, I don't think so," another gasped. "She looks too real to be making believe."

Laurie Phillips *is* real. She was, on that April day, an intensely disturbed nine-year-old—one of the four million deeply troubled children in America who have no place to go. Not sufficiently psychotic, she could expect no place at a state mental institution. Not retarded, she could get no help at a special school for the mentally deficient. Not criminal, she could find no haven at a girls' training school. But the public schools could not cope with her, psychiatric clinics had neither space nor time to undertake the difficult treatment, and privately engaged child psychiatrists had got nowhere.

Most such children, frequently characterized as "unmotivated for therapy," remain at home, where they deteriorate, or they are sloughed off to custodial institutions, where they wither away in different fashion. There are too few professionals with sufficient boldness, patience and empathy to treat these profoundly disturbed youngsters.

In a last desperate effort to find help for Laurie, her mother was taking her to the Montanari Residential Treatment Center and Clinical School in Hialeah, Florida. Here they would find a man who, though neither psychiatrist, nor psychologist, nor social worker, had achieved remarkable results with these disturbed children.

Adelio Giuseppe Ambruano Pasquale Antonio Montanari, known more affectionately as Monty, would seem an unlikely person to take on such a task. He is a handsome, chunky, powerfully built man in his middle forties who combines the physique of a former football player with the gentle manner of a minister. He speaks in the bluntly coarse vernacular of the man in the street rather than in the jargon of the professional. He is casual, accepting and manipulative, while appearing to be ingenuous.

A maverick in the field, he scorns all the trappings of the professional and is most comfortable when exchanging grins and conversation with his young charges. Seated at his desk, peering over the straight tops of the Ben Franklin spectacles that sit awkwardly on the tip of his nose, he is far less at ease.

His unique abilities stem not so much from academic training—he possesses only a BS in education—as from his own life experiences. His personal knowledge of emotional disturbance allows him to operate on the same wavelength as that of a disturbed child and satisfies a deeply ingrained need to heal such children in order to heal himself. From this need derives the drive that makes his work not merely his occupation, but his preoccupation, and serves to make his facilities, his staff and his young charges mere extensions of himself.

Remembering the childhood experiences that made him feel like a pariah, he is able to identify and "tune in" with other little pariahs, drawing upon his own intuitive resources and the gist of his academic experience to make understanding them possible. He might fairly be likened to the alcoholic who cures himself and then must go on to cure others in order to validate the cure. On another level, he is like the psychiatrist who undergoes the experience of the "consciousness-expanding" drugs such as LSD to permit himself a glimpse of a sick world in order better to understand its inhabitants.

Laurie Phillips was to be Monty's greatest challenge. She offered him a further chance to prove himself and to attain recognition in that select circle of professional people who questioned his unorthodox methods. He is the sort of man whose incentive increases in proportion to the challenge.

Experts on child behavior agree that it is not uncommon for youngsters to assume animal mannerisms in occasional flights into fantasy, but Laurie Phillips' behavior had reached the level of the bizarre.

Laurie's soaring imagination and fragile sensitivity had, for a long time, disguised what was happening to her. Actually, her transformation had taken a young lifetime.

Laurie began with all the so-called advantages: a comfortable suburban house, a father who was successful in business, a young and intelligent mother, and an agile mind and body that enabled her to speak her first words and take her first steps before her first birthday.

But Laurie's presence in the home aroused her father's jealousy and eventually affected the relationship between her parents. "My husband didn't like to share my attention with anyone else," Mrs. Phillips recalls. "He often took out his feelings on our dog, and sometimes on Laurie."

When the dog was punished, he would run for cover under the kitchen table and Laurie began to emulate the pet of whom she was so fond. She, too, began to enjoy hiding under tables.

As the hostilities within the family increased, Mr. Phillips drew further and further apart from his wife and abandoned the rough-and-tumble games he once played with Laurie. Perhaps to compensate for this lack of attention, Laurie began to demonstrate an unusual compassion for animals, reaching out eagerly to care for stray dogs that wandered through the back yard. When she was not permitted to bring them into the house, she threw violent temper tantrums.

In an attempt to soothe her feelings, her father said that he would buy her a big cuddly Irish setter, a breed which she especially admired. "But he never kept his promise," Mrs. Phillips says bitterly, "and when Laurie reached school age, he wanted to send her away to boarding school."

This was Mr. Phillips' final desperate attempt at regaining his wife's total allegiance, but by then the marriage had run its course. All that had kept it going to this point was the individual interest of the parents in their own respective careers, for Mrs. Phillips also was successful in business.

When the marriage finally sputtered into divorce, Mrs. Phillips' preoccupation with both her personal and her business life prevented her from noticing her daughter's increasing and obsessive involvement with animals and her subtle, gradual disintegration.

Family and friends considered it "cute" when they overheard Laurie "talking" to dogs. They smiled when she explained, "People learn foreign languages. Why not dog language? I guess because it takes a lot of work to try to understand them."

Laurie was reaching out for understanding, but no one realized it, even when she took on the specific canine characteristics of barking and whimpering and wrinkling her nose.

"She has such a wonderful imagination," her mother says, "that we thought what she was doing was all in fun. She used to laugh and we laughed with her."

Her schoolteachers were equally unobservant, misled by Laurie's "very superior" IQ rating and her outstanding grades. Even when they caught her growling at her classmates in the schoolyard, they dismissed her behavior as not atypical. "All children think they are animals when they are very young," Mrs. Phillips remembers being told by one teacher during openschool week. They advised her not to be alarmed, saying, "She'll outgrow it."

They overlooked the many drawings of dogs in Laurie's notebook and the scribbled comments in the margin: "Dogs are nicer than people." They overlooked the frequent references to younger children, especially boys, as "pussycats," the natural enemies of dogs, and disregarded her tormenting of such youngsters. They overlooked these eccentricities because, somehow, she continued to function academically, thereby drawing attention away from her emotional difficulties.

By the time Laurie reached the fourth grade, she was slipping in and out of her fantasy world more frequently. Still it was almost impossible to tell when she was playing and when she was acting compulsively. Only when the outbursts of temper and destructiveness became more frequent, and when she could no longer control her impulse to kick, scream and smash things during one of her rages, did her mother become fearful that Laurie would not "outgrow it" without assistance.

Mrs. Phillips sought psychiatric help to correct Laurie's antisocial behavior. Three times a week her child visited a psychiatrist. One month went by, then two, then three. The child was not responding to treatment. On the contrary, she became more and more aggressive. She bit and scratched her aunt and uncle, threatened to jump out of a window and, for her own safety, had to be tied to a chair on a number of occasions. Thoroughly frightened and quite desperate, Mrs. Phillips took Laurie to the Menninger Clinic in Topeka, Kansas, for psychiatric evaluation.

After five days of tests and interviews, the doctors at Menninger warned that Laurie was in danger of abandoning the last hold on reality unless intensive therapy away from her home environment was started at once and continued for several years. The gloomy prognosis was brightened only by the fact that Laurie had considerable strength of spirit, a result of her basic closeness to her mother, that might help to pull her through.

But Mrs. Phillips could not afford lengthy treatments, which cost up to $15,000 a year because of the high proportion of professional staff to patients.

Frantically, she sought help at other leading residential-treatment centers throughout the nation. "It was futile," she says. "For months we went everywhere. Either there was no room, or Laurie was 'too disturbed,' or else they were so cold and businesslike. They just didn't seem to really care what was happening to my little girl. She was deteriorating in front of my eyes and nobody did anything."

She sought the guidance of the one doctor who had not been "cold and businesslike." He was Dr. Povl W. Tousseing of the

Children's Division at Menninger, a big, smiling, soft-spoken man of Danish extraction with a deep affection for children. It was he who suggested Montanari.

"Some psychiatrists look down their noses at him because he doesn't have a lot of diplomas on his walls," Dr. Tousseing told her, "while others refer their most difficult patients to him. He takes on children whom others would feel hopeless about, including some who have murdered and solicited. He is a very gutsy guy who will fight for his young patients, a gifted person who does not pretend to be a psychiatrist but who uses a more intuitive approach than the average psychiatrist. And the secret of his success seems to be this intuitive approach, this ability to charm children."

Moreover, the fee at the Montanari Treatment Center was only three hundred dollars a month, probably the lowest in the field. And although Montanari is not a doctor himself, Mrs. Phillips learned, he does have a hard core of professional psychiatrists, psychologists, physicians, psychiatric nurses and social workers who work with his staff. But at the center of the therapeutic team is Monty himself.

He differs from most others in the field because he displays little interest either in the fundamental causes of emotional maladjustment or in their degree, and even refuses to divulge such information to his staff. "Let's say, for example," he explains, "that a boy has homosexual tendencies. The staff might interpret every sign of affection from that boy as an indication of such tendencies. But it's the need for affection of a healthy kind that is driving that boy the wrong way sex-wise. It would be pretty sad if his perfectly normal demands for love were misinterpreted. The same problem, in a different way, came up with Laurie. If the staff knew everything about her background, they might blame her sickness on her mother or her father. But that's only half the story and, besides, she has to go back home to her mother, you see. So I don't believe in reinforcing such notions. I like my staff to come to their own conclusions after working with the child. And you'd be surprised how many times all the testing that went on before just doesn't hold up when the child is treated only as a sick little boy or girl, not as the clinical average of a bunch of professional opinions. I mean, we know that he or she is a misfit, or else the child wouldn't be here in the first place."

By the time Laurie arrived at the Montanari Clinical School, she was much worse than when Dr. Tousseing had seen her in Topeka. "She had shrunk from seventy to fifty-five pounds," Monty recalls. "She had taken an awful beating in those few months and was walking a hairline. She wouldn't talk at all. She ate, slept, walked, howled, barked and bit exactly like a little dog."

When he saw her for the first time at Miami Airport, he admits to being shocked. Mrs. Phillips kept repeating, "Oh, God, oh, God, can this be happening to me?" and handed her daughter over to Monty with great relief.

Monty hustled Laurie into his waiting station wagon and, while a member of his staff drove them to the school, he removed her leash. "I had to make her understand that I would accept her and love her no matter how she behaved," he explains. "When she bit me"—his arms and hands still bear scars of her teeth marks—"I wouldn't let on that it hurt. I kept telling her, 'Laurie, it doesn't make any difference to me if you don't want to act like a little girl. I'll let you *act* like a dog if you want, but I won't let you *be* a dog.' "

Monty subscribes to the belief that an emotionally disturbed child is no different from other children except that such a child's desires and urges are stronger and, therefore, less easily masked.

"I had a feeling I could help Laurie," he says. "Little dog or not, she wasn't psychotic. Lots of people in the field wouldn't touch her because she was so sick. She didn't fit into a mold, and there was no guarantee that they would succeed with her. But that's what made her somebody special. She just wasn't any child, you see. Any fool can work with just any child, but with someone like Laurie, you have to work a hell of a lot harder. You have to pour in everything you've got and then some."

Here, in Laurie Phillips, was a major test of his ability and his ideas of therapy and reeducation. As soon as they arrived at the school he began putting these ideas to work. He sent Mrs.

Phillips away to her hotel, and led Laurie into his small private office, closing the door behind him.

Now quite suddenly, her mother gone, the rest of the world closed off, Laurie ceased to bark and snap. Monty went to his desk but watched her out of the corner of his eye. Quietly, she withdrew to a corner, her head hung low like a dispirited cur. Sitting on her "haunches," knees bent, with her hands stretched out before her, she growled now and then in a mournful manner.

For eight hours she sat in that position, never moving, never looking up, while Monty, seemingly oblivious of her presence, went about his business. He did his paper work, spoke on the telephone and talked with other children or members of his staff who dropped in at the office.

This apparent lack of attention was Monty's way of showing Laurie that he accepted her as she was, or as she pretended to be. For he did not treat her like a little dog, which to all intents and purposes she was, nor like a little girl, which she was not as far as her behavior was concerned. He treated her simply as a little girl who was insisting on being treated like a dog, and let her sit at his feet.

The following day, Monty tried to get Laurie to talk to Dr. Evan Katz, his director of psychiatric services, and Dr. William P. Albaugh, his director of psychological services, but she would not allow them to approach her, and growled menacingly when they came near. They could only observe her from a polite distance and were forced to make their diagnoses from these remote observations and a careful examination of her records.

Dr. Katz described her illness as "severe childhood schizophrenia, an absence of logical thinking." He told Monty, "Orthodox therapy can't possibly reach her. In order to divest herself of her symptoms, she has to be reached in an unclinical atmosphere by a human being with whom she can develop a trusting relationship. Her problems are so severe that contact with her family now would be impractical. The staff must become her family until she is redeveloped emotionally. And from the look of things, you're the one to whom she seems to relate best."

Dr. Albaugh, in his report, said, "It isn't the role she assumes that is paramount, but the role she rejects. She just does not trust humans and, until she does, she will prefer to remain a dog. If you can develop your relationship with her and continue to feel comfortable with her intense hostility, you might win her back to the human race."

This was easier said than done. After Mrs. Phillips left, Laurie's behavior deteriorated to the point that she refused to eat. Whenever Monty and his staff approached with food, they were met with angry growls. Monty insisted that she would eat when she became hungry enough. But after five days of fasting, she was beginning to show signs of dehydration and the school's pediatrician wanted to take drastic measures. Anxious to avoid such a procedure, Monty tried rubbing a piece of steak back and forth across Laurie's lips, then setting it on a dish under the table. As he turned away, Laurie leaped for the meat, taking it between her "paws" and gnawing it ravenously. From that moment on, a dish under the table became her regular dinner plate.

"I decided," Monty says, "that if this was the only way she'd eat, this is how we'd have to feed her. It was the same thing with getting her to drink liquids. If we asked her, 'Laurie, are you thirsty?' she'd slump down in a corner like a sulky dog with its tail between its legs. But we found that when we changed the question to a command and said, 'Laurie, you look thirsty, come have some water,' she'd follow obediently on all fours and lap up the water from the glass with her tongue."

Visitors expressed shock and revulsion at seeing the child taking food and drink in this manner. "They said it wasn't normal," Monty recalls, "but I told them, goddamn it, this little girl *isn't* normal. In order to make her normal, according to my philosophy, you have to feed her needs. And at that time, these were her needs. I wasn't interested in teaching her table manners. I didn't care how she ate just as long as she ate. She was not ready to be taught anything yet. She had to feel accepted before she felt like learning. I had to reach her before I could teach her."

During the period when Laurie was at her worst, Dr. Tousseing visited the Clinical School as part of the in-service training program that made the experience of trained professional people available to the lay members of the staff. "It was astonishing," he says, "to see how this child would sit in Montanari's office for hours at a time while he carried on with his work, breaking away now and then nonchalantly to take the child out, whenever she wet or soiled herself, and change her."

This matter-of-fact approach was Monty's way of expressing respect for Laurie as a person without demanding that she conform to normal rules. In return, she would allow him the privilege of brushing her hair and bathing her.

She would have nothing to do with the other children, preferring to trot in lonesome circles in the play yard. The children were discouraged from whistling at her, since this strengthened her fantasy and brought more snaps, snarls and even bites. For a similar reason, dogs were denied to her as playmates, for she would chase them, sniff at them and maul them so ardently that they would flee from her.

To give her contact with the community, Monty let her follow him to the luncheonette, the supermarket and the barbershop. She walked sometimes on her "hind legs," sometimes on "all fours." When a curious passerby would stop to ask about her strange behavior, Monty would shrug and say, "This is a little girl who wants to be a dog."

On several occasions, Monty took her to his home for dinner with his family. At these times, Laurie would grab her plate between her teeth, remove it from the table, carry it to a distant corner and then eat quietly in her doglike fashion.

The family watched in silent amazement as Laurie used her nose to turn the light switch on and off, scratched with her "paws" to open the door, and slept on a newspaper on the floor.

On Mother's Day, when Monty asked Laurie if she would like to telephone her mother in Los Angeles, she cried dry tears. In an effort to get her to speak, he asked her the phone number. She replied by barking the correct number of times. "Well, if you'd like to call her, you can," he said, "but you'll have to make the call yourself." She did, dialing the number with a pencil held between her teeth. On hearing her mother's voice, she barked joyfully but still would not speak.

Monty did not press her further except to remind her casually, "You know, honey, the sooner you start talking, the sooner you can go home." He was trying to motivate her and, although she did not answer, he saw that she listened attentively.

Five weeks after her arrival at the Clinical School, Laurie was still snapping and growling but was no longer biting. She had begun to read a book about animals, holding the book between her "paws" while stretched out on the floor on her stomach. Her teacher would pick up the book when Laurie wasn't reading and place it on her desk, tacitly encouraging her to sit in class with the other children. Shortly thereafter, Laurie did join the class. She also began to sleep in her bed and to allow her house mother to spoon-feed her at the table. The painstaking, subtle acceptance practiced by Monty and his staff was beginning to weaken Laurie's hold on fantasy, and their attempts to wean her away from her canine alter ego grew bolder.

Before another month went by, she was improving in many directions, and Monty says, "We could see that we were getting through to her, that she was getting better. She was still growling but I think that was only to uphold her reputation. She'd begun to show some faith in people again but we had to be careful not to expect too much too soon."

He considered it a good sign when she started to put her feelings down on paper. She wrote a story about a dog that was "sorrowful and broken-spirited, the pet of the kennel because of the clownish way he acted whenever he knew people were watching, terribly lonely and sad because his master and mistress gave him food and shelter, but he didn't know whether they loved him, disliked him or hated him." Monty sensed her need for self-expression and used this need to motivate her use of a desk and a pencil.

Laurie now accepted a glass of water in her hands instead of lapping it up with her tongue from the floor. She was still not able to hold the glass securely because her fingers, twisted into "paws" for so long, were stiff, but when the water spilled she whined like a child instead of whimpering like a dog.

During this period, she laughed, for the first time, when one of the children took a spill. To an outsider this may have seemed cruel, but to the delighted staff it indicated progress, for this was her first expression of anything except anger or complete detachment.

At the Montanari family dinner table one evening, Monty set her plate before her and said, "There's your dinner, Laurie. If you're hungry, go on and eat." He said nothing more, proceeding with his own meal along with his family. For a long moment, Laurie hesitated, but seeing that nobody was paying attention to her, she picked up her knife and fork and started to eat.

"We were all so excited," Monty recalls with a grin, "that we wanted to get up and cheer. But we kept still. We didn't dare make a big thing out of this, you see. We had to accept improvements in her behavior the same way we accepted everything else about her. Otherwise she'd think she was getting better just to please us, and not herself."

Another turning point came a few weeks later. A child teased Laurie and she bit, though not hard. When the other child did not bite back, Laurie spoke her first words: "You idiot!"

The children immediately began to chant, "Laurie's talking! Laurie's talking!" She then refused to say another word.

"When the kids made such a fuss over her talking," Monty says, "two things happened. One was that Laurie knew that somebody else liked her, that she wasn't alone anymore. The other thing was that she wasn't yet ready to become one of them. She was starting to show some faith in adults but she still didn't trust other children. So she pulled away and stopped talking to get them off her back."

Monty was scheduled to speak at the University of North Carolina in Chapel Hill at about this time. He knew the speech represented an important step toward recognition, but he hesitated to leave Laurie now that he felt that the breakthrough was near. "I was pretty upset, too," he recalls, "because a couple of psychiatrists came by, spent half an hour or so looking around and criticized everything."

He contacted his good friend Dr. Tousseing at the Menninger Clinic, and felt reassured when Dr. Tousseing wrote back:

The good news about Laurie has brought some sorely needed relief to all of us here who are rooting for this child. While your projected one-week absence probably will set her back a bit, I am sure now that she will get over this and again gain confidence in the environment enough to interact with it. This does not mean that there isn't going to be a long road ahead, but at least it will be a lot easier to live with the child and to give to her. As for those psychiatrists who tore into you and your program, they must have not understood what you are trying to do because, I can assure you, I have not tried to be gentle on you. But I have also been tooting your horn, and I think a lot of people here will be interested in getting to know you better. I hope that you will try to visit us here and, though I know you won't approve of them, we would still like to show you our new facilities!

Monty was unable to travel to Menninger but he did go to Chapel Hill, where he lectured on emotional disturbance among children. When questioned about his methodology, he said:

I'm an educator, not a doctor. We're mavericks, you see, and we're off bounds with some of the traditional ways of doing things. We have a different philosophy about our kids, we don't look at them from a clinical standpoint. They're human beings, no different from the rest of God's children. We aren't pious and we aren't do-gooders. To us, a child is a child, and you have to adapt what you know to fit their needs, not yours, and then you'll be successful. Right now I have a little girl who thought she was a dog. And I've been successful with her because I lay on the floor under the table with her, three or four hours a day sometimes, down to her level, and we barked and we played dog and cat and she chased me around the office. Undignified? Sure, but I'm reaching her. And you know something? I had a good time!

When he returned to Hialeah, he crept up behind Laurie, poked her gently in the ribs and said, "Who is it?" She turned and said, "Hi," then checked herself. Monty pursued his advantage. "I know you want to talk, Laurie," he said, "but I don't care whether you do or not. If you really want to talk to me, we'll keep it a secret. Or maybe you'd like to call your mother and talk to her?"

Laurie threw her arms around him impulsively and began to cry. This time the tears were real. It was her first show of affection. Now, after three months of silence, she began to talk without letup.

"She began to get better," Monty explains, "when she realized she wasn't always playacting and that it was getting harder and harder for her to come out of her state. This was an important element of her obsession. Her fear of losing her ability to be a little dog or a little girl at will was really greater than her fear of humans. So now we had to strengthen her wish to remain a human being."

He involved himself even more directly and more personally with Laurie, had soul-searching conversations with her, often squatting beside her on the floor of her cottage when the other children were out at play. A sample of one of these conversations was recorded on tape.

"Laurie, sometimes I wish I'd have taken pictures of you when you used to run around like a little dog," Monty began earnestly. "Remember when I sat here with you, and Dr. Tousseing heard me say 'goddamnit' and wondered what kind of a man I am, because men aren't supposed to use language like that, honey? I didn't mean for anybody to hear me but I said words like that because I was so upset about you. I worried about going off on a trip because I didn't want you to feel hurt, but I had a feeling you'd be all right, you see, Laurie?"

She answered in a small, tight voice. "Yes, but now that I'm not a dog anymore, I don't want any other human to know I'm getting better."

"Why? Do you enjoy being a dog, honey? Or do you want to go home to your mama and play with other children like a little girl, hm?"

"But they tease me."

"Now, honey, I know they tease you but you tease them, too. Like when a little girl says, 'Laurie, please play with me,' and you go, 'Arf, arf!' and start snapping and growling."

"No one ever said that to me, that they wanted to play with me."

"Sure they have, Laurie. But lots of times they don't say it in words, they don't have to say it in words. Lots of the children have been dying to be your friends but I've been holding them back, you see, because I didn't think you were ready to make friends."

"Well, I don't want to be friends with any other human except you, Monty, because one minute they're your friends and the next minute they're not friends. They're not normal."

"Tell me, Laurie, do you . . . do you want to be normal?"

"Well, it's normal of me to want dogs because I love dogs."

"I love dogs, too, honey, and all kinds of animals. You know that big old catfish I've got? You saw that big old catfish in my pool at home."

"A fish can't be a pal."

"Sure he can. Why, every time I go out, that old catfish, he looks at me, he knows just when I'm going to feed him. And I have a couple of ducks, too, that are my friends. Every time they see me, they go 'Quack, quack,' and I get a big kick out of it."

"Yes, but they can't be with you all the time because they need water. Not like a dog."

"But Laurie, honey, the way you were behaving, not even a dog wanted to come to you. Remember that old mutt that needed a friend, remember him? He was mangy, underfed, nobody gave a damn about him, nobody wanted him. You could have been his friend but he didn't like the way you were playing with him and he ran away. Now, if you act like a lady, you can have all the friends, all the dogs you want, you see?"

The daily dialogues continued as Monty soothed her with understanding and hope, encouraging her to completely discard her canine alter ego. "I knew I was getting somewhere," he says with a fond smile, "when Laurie began writing to her mama about how much she disliked being here."

One of these letters to her mother reads: "I hate it here. There's no reason for me to be here anymore unless you make me stay. I've learned to be a person."

Less than five months after her admission to the Clinical School—several years short of the minimum time which other professionals had estimated—she was sufficiently recovered to be enrolled in the fifth grade of the local public school while continuing to live and receive care at Montanari's. She achieved straight A's on her report card. She was back to seventy pounds, looking pretty and feminine again, her voice no longer deep and husky but pleasantly childlike.

Very much aware of her past illness and proud of her recovery, her remarkable insight into "the time I was a little dog," as she puts it, shines through a poem she wrote after giving up her obsession. In these verses, which she entitles "Memories of the Faithful," she reveals her great hunger for love and understanding, for the "doggy" of the poem is, of course, Laurie herself.

> Oh doggy, oh doggy,
>   Never did I know
> How much I really loved you
>   Till I had to see you go.
>
> You were my faithful companion
>   Every day of my life,
> You stayed with me through thick and thin
>   And through my hour of strife.
>
> You never seemed to notice
>   If I were cruel or mean,
> You just had to stick with me,
>   That was the way it seemed.
>
> Way up there in Heaven,
>   I'll meet you there someday,
> And we will be together
>   To romp again and play.
>
> Oh doggy, oh doggy,
>   Never did I know
> How much I really loved you
>   Till I had to see you go.

Laurie is home again now and her mother has great hopes for her. "She won't be ordinary when she grows up," she says. "I have a feeling that one day she'll do something really great." She already has. She has become a little girl.

Monty ascribes his success with Laurie to the "formula" upon which he predicates all his treatment. "She just had to be re-educated emotionally, socially and academically, in that order," he says. "We had to come in through the back door to reach her. That's the formula we follow with all our kids, except that our techniques vary with each child. You can't treat them all alike because emotional disturbance is a very individual thing. What works for one may not work at all for another. So we try something else. And if we have to break the rules to cure the sickness, well, we just goddamn well break them, that's all."

II

MONTANARI TALKS, THINKS AND ACTS like a man who refuses to be bound by rules when they interfere with the exercise of his deepest feelings. He is direct, audacious and self-serving when he feels he has to be, when the welfare of the children to whom he refers as "my kids" is concerned. He thinks nothing of shocking a visitor, civic or professional, by lifting a squealing child high in his arms and remarking, "Mama had to peddle herself to keep this little fellow here. She's too proud to take charity. Or maybe she feels guilty for her child turning out this way. But you know something? You've got to admire a woman like that."

As a result, he has been written off, privately or publicly, by some of his more genteel colleagues in the field as a mere upstart, an illiterate in the world of troubled children. Yet even his most ardent detractors are unable to explain away the results he has obtained with utterly rejected children—he calls them "the kids nobody wants"—whom others could not or would not reclaim.

His success rating is very high, almost 70 percent. Because of the severity of their emotional disorders, his young charges may not be completely cured but most are able to function and many go on to marry and raise families. He defines a minimal success as "a child who can attend public school without too much furor and live in the community without too much disturbance," and takes pains to explain, "I am not a miracle worker. Some of my kids are just too far gone. If they reach my standards for minimal success, that's a big accomplishment for them."

He has his boosters as well as his detractors. Mrs. Louise Alpert, casework supervisor of the Children's Service Bureau in Dade County, sent her daughter to work at the Montanari Clinical School in preparation for a future in social work. She says, "That man has something to give children that few others have. We've sent him a dozen youngsters who weren't ready for public school or foster-home placement and there was only one he couldn't help at all."

Judge Ben J. Sheppard, senior judge of Dade County Juvenile Court and a practicing pediatrician, says, "I've seen kids that *nobody* else would touch except Monty and I've seen him take those kids and turn them into human beings."

At this writing, Monty has in his charge 155 intensely disturbed boys and girls, some as young as five, a few as old as eighteen. Many are indigent, and are supported by contributions from public and family agencies, or by private scholarships donated by generous individuals, civic groups and service clubs. These youngsters come not only from the community, the county and the state, but from a dozen other states and three foreign countries as well. All but a handful reside on the premises, for the first step in treatment is separation from the disturbing environment. They are referred by physicians, psychiatrists, psychologists, various agencies, the juvenile courts, other treatment centers that cannot cope with them, and the parents of former "pupils."

The atmosphere in which they live—working, playing, learning, trying to get the feel of life, sometimes for the first time—is geared for growth. In a tropical setting of palm trees and ever-present sunshine are twelve cottages. The houses are located on several streets in a beautiful residential area, extending from North to South Fourth Street and from Second to Fourth Avenue in the heart of Hialeah.

The ranch-style white stucco cottages with their bright-red doors are functional but attractive, sturdily constructed, lined with windows, air-conditioned and spotlessly clean. Each cottage has its own living room and modern kitchen and the homey dormitories are tastefully furnished in maple. There is no clutter, no bric-a-brac to impress parents, no distractions to confuse the child who longs for and can only contend with surroundings of utter simplicity. There are no locked doors, no "quiet rooms," but there are extensive yards to play in. A halfway house for children preparing to return home, a central administrative unit and three separate schools—one for boys, one for girls and one for the very young of both sexes—complete the setting.

At a distance, these disturbed youngsters might be mistaken for one's own, but up close the resemblance vanishes. The lovable five-year-old so busy finger-painting is using his feces for paint. The adorable titian-haired teen-ager who runs up to embrace a visitor hugs hard enough to all but break the astonished newcomer's bones. The handsome sun-tanned eleven-year-old boy who scampers to the top of the Florida holly tree is actually intent on reaching the moon in order to escape reality.

Any morning, when the early haze has not yet lifted, the small, earnest voices of still sleepy children can be heard whining, pleading, prattling: "My blouse, won't somebody help me find my blouse, oh please please please?" . . . "Someone wet my bed last night, what an awful bitchy thing to do!" . . . "You're a slob, a blob, a glob glob glob." The sounds of awakening, but of a special quality, with an extravagance of tone and feeling that is characteristic of the disturbed child.

At nightfall, the darkness of the hour seems to merge with the darkness of the mind and the sounds take on a new dimension. The nightmare world of the troubled children becomes inhabited by shrill ghosts and the fantasizing goes far beyond the ordinary make-believe of normal children. A madonna-like thirteen-year-old who has sat immobilized all day, with a foolish smile across her face and her eyes glazed, suddenly begins to weep uncontrollably and to whine for comfort. A husky fifteen-year-old becomes enraged by a crease in the otherwise smooth bed sheet, snatches a lamp from a table and smashes it furiously to the floor to indicate his displeasure. A twelve-year-old freckle-faced boy screams for attention from his cottage mates, rocking

wildly back and forth on his bed as he shouts, "Look, I'm screw-
ing a girl, ha ha ha!"

Monty says, "These kids aren't products of hell. They're just
sick little kids who need help because somebody let them down
or because something they were born with made them different
from other kids or maybe because they had a sickness that damaged their brain power. So they're frustrated, mixed up and act
out their hates and fears. They're easily hurt because they can
sense things your normal children can't sense. They're hard to
handle and hard to teach, but somebody's got to try or they'll
end up in straitjackets, or in jail, or as 'vegetables.'"

Along with the professionals who serve on his staff, Monty
has ninety full-time and fourteen part-time employees: teachers,
house parents, occupational and speech therapists, supervisors,
principals, maids and maintenance workers. These people supply
the blood and guts of Monty's operation. Like their director,
most lack impressive academic backgrounds, but they all exhibit
in great measure the qualities of devotion, understanding, frustration tolerance, ingenuity and insight.

"We often take a youngster home, same as Monty does," says
one staff member, "to see how the child adjusts in a family setting."

This sort of personal involvement is part of the reeducation
process practiced at Montanari's. Several staff members have
gone so far as to become foster parents, allowing some of the
children to live with them in order to continue therapy around
the clock.

"Every child has to relate to somebody," Monty points out.
"If it isn't me, it's one of my teachers, or a house parent. One
child related best to the maid who cleaned up her cottage. And
when a child gets all he can out of such a relationship, we set
up another, then another, and another. It's a dynamic process.
This is how we bring the child back into society."

Another aspect of this "milieu therapy," as it is sometimes
called, is the "mixing" of children. The personality-damaged,
the brain-damaged and the intellectually damaged live, play
and work side by side. They look after one another, learn acceptance from their peers and go outside their nonclinical surround-

ings—even the nurse is not allowed to dress in medical white—
to visit the shops, the theaters and the recreational facilities of
the community.

For Monty does not believe in shielding his children from
social contact. He even permits outside visitors to come in and
meet the children, something few if any treatment centers allow.

"I want to expose my kids to people," he explains, "so that
they won't feel different. I want to get them out into the community because that's where they're going to have to live and
get along. In addition to having to learn to live with themselves, they have to be able to live with other people, and that
includes their parents. You'd be surprised how many parents
refuse to cooperate. So I've got to help their kids to cope with
their parents. That's why my place has to be situated in the
middle of everything. It's a whole lot easier to bring movies
in to the kids, but it's better for them to go to the local movie
theater."

So he takes them to the local theater; he takes them to their
churches; he gives them small allowances and takes them to the
stores. He encourages them when they are ready to mingle with
"normal" neighborhood children. He takes advantage of the
many public facilities: swimming pools, beach and play areas,
out-patient clinics and public schools for those children who
are ready for them. Visiting psychiatrists and psychologists at-
tribute much of Montanari's success to this repeated contact
with community life. At the same time, the availability of neighborhood public facilities keeps the cost of treatment down so
that the community aspect of the Montanari method has practical as well as therapeutic significance.

When Monty established his Clinical School in 1952, he did
so out of impatience with traditional techniques, standards that
he considered unrealistic and "the endless array of tests, professional double-talk and time-consuming red tape" that he felt
impressed everyone except the children concerned. His notions
on reclaiming such children stem from his own life experiences.
Like his children, he has always gone against the grain of life.
"I had a rough time as a kid," he confesses. "I was a poor reader

and couldn't concentrate on anything very long. My parents were pretty strict and I guess I rebelled at their rigidity."

He was born on May 25, 1917, in Winchendon, Massachusetts, a hilly, wooded country town to which some hundred families had emigrated from the region of Fano, Italy. The Italians settled on the outskirts of the town in a kind of ghetto and were referred to by the Yankee, Irish and French-Canadian population as "that happy family of wops." All of the Italians worked at the local cotton mill, rented their homes from their employer and gratefully accepted any gestures of paternalism that were offered to them.

Monty's father had a greater social conscience than the others and a high regard for the values of his new country. He helped to initiate a night school to teach English to the Italian-speaking population and to prepare them for American citizenship. He borrowed ideas from the *cooperativa* of Italy in organizing his countrymen into a collective buying group that would eliminate the profits of the middleman who sold them grapes for their wine, flour for their bread and cheese for their pasta.

From such an inheritance, Monty derives his own strong social sense. Although shy by nature, he rose above his timidity during his high-school years and engaged in lively debate on social issues. He became popular as the school's "most outspoken liberal," yet was able to remain on good terms with the arch-conservatives with whom he debated. Again and again, he argued that "the troubles of one member of a group are the troubles of the whole society."

From his earliest years, he was encouraged by his parents to fight with words and ideas rather than with his fists. If he was caught resorting to fisticuffs, he was punished severely and threatened with reform school. From this stringent attitude grew a fear of policemen and authority in general.

He was made to meet higher standards of behavior and accomplishment than the other Italian boys. When he fell short, he was punished frequently by being sent to his room and made to eat a raw onion, which he despised, but his respect for his parents was too great to permit him to rebel. He ate the onions, while the tears streamed down his cheeks.

Monty was very close to his mother and was often called "mama's boy" by his friends. A short, slight woman who worked long hours at the cotton mill to help support Monty and his younger sister, his mother was usually gentle but there were times when she would become angry and slap young Monty hard across his face with her *verghetta,* a massive wedding ring made from an Italian gold coin. He would reel out the front door only to return, seconds later, through the rear door, grinning ingenuously and calling, "Hi, Mama." He could not fight back at her the way his sister did.

Monty was tractable, and his tractability resulted in his following the dictates of his father, who longed for him to rise above the working class. He spurned the attitude of his fellow Italians, who dropped out of high school at sixteen to take jobs at the mill. Instead, he remained in school, working part-time, to become the first of the Italian community to be graduated.

But there were emotional repercussions which he thinks stemmed from his mixed feelings toward his family and from a growing feeling of inadequacy because he was "different." Unable to confide his deepest thoughts to either parent, he sought out a teacher, an attractive young woman to whom he related emotionally as an adolescent as well as intellectually as a student.

"I became his confidante," recalls the teacher, Mrs. Robert Montague of Southbridge, Massachusetts. "Monty—we used to call him Adelio, or Del, then—used to stay after school to pour out his pent-up feelings. He was terribly afraid of letting his father down because he knew how strongly his father felt about his going to college and learning a profession. But Del was undisciplined as a student. He preferred to help other, less capable classmates make the grade than to put his energies into advancing himself. He was at his best when he found a cause to fight for. But a good deal of the time, he was terribly depressed and came to me for a pickup. I didn't suspect then that he would one day pour his energies into helping disturbed children but I knew that somehow he would wind up fighting for the underdog."

Monty's father selected Antioch College in Yellow Springs,

Ohio, because it was known as a liberal institution. Monty was accepted but the going proved difficult. "I just couldn't concentrate," he remembers. "I'd go to the college library and try to stay glued to a book. I'd keep saying to myself, 'This time, goddamn it, you're going to do it,' but pretty soon I'd either fall asleep or have to get up and take a walk."

He questioned everything they taught him, even the principles of Freud. When his psychology class studied the movements of a white rat in a maze, he remained unimpressed and shocked his professor by commenting disdainfully, "Big deal! So OK, you have a rat and he runs through a maze to find a piece of cheese. So what? What have you done? You don't have to prove something like this, it's self-evident. You take any poor little rat and starve him to death, then goose him in the ass to push him along to find food, and what do you think he's going to do? If you're hungry, you're going to find food, that's just natural. That's second nature, survival of the fittest. So this whole thing is just a waste of time."

He flunked the psychology course and had to repeat it. Then, as part of the work-study plan of the curriculum, he was sent to Chicago to work at a settlement house, for he had decided to major in social work. But here, too, he could not restrain his natural impulse to speak up at what he considered injustice.

A seven-year-old boy, abandoned by his mother, was brought to the settlement house by a policeman. When the mother was finally located and the boy returned to her, Monty became furious with the director.

"I told him that I thought what he was doing was all wrong," he says, recalling the incident. "It just didn't make sense to me to send that little boy back to his mama, who obviously didn't want him. And the director got awful mad at me, said I wasn't qualified and that he knew what he was doing. The more he said, the madder I got. So he threw me out of there."

After three years at Antioch, he was cut loose, a failure. Rather than face his family, whom he knew he had disappointed, he attempted suicide. But the suicide attempt failed, probably because he was not fully committed to it, and he swallowed his pride and his anguish and went home.

Co-op stores were popular at the time and Monty understood their operation because he had a good business sense. He worked at several stores in a number of cities until World War II broke out. Eager to escape from the business world and contribute his services, he tried to enlist in the Navy but was rejected because of a torn knee cartilage stemming from a boyhood accident. He did succeed in enlisting in the Army and seized the first opportunity to enroll in Officers' Candidate School. He worked hard to make the grade but was washed out.

"It was the first time in my life I really wanted anything and really worked hard to get it," he says. "It made me pretty mad when they dumped me, because I felt I could do better than many of the guys who had passed. It bothered me a lot."

He was bothered enough to look into himself, and he realized that somewhere, deep inside him, something rebelled at being an officer. He felt more comfortable with the regular enlisted men. Chastened by this self-discovery and his rejection, he began to fight back. He was promoted to sergeant and put in charge of a gunnery class. He proved to be a great teacher and began to find his own success in the success of his least artful students. For the first time, he became aware that by building the egos of others, he could build his own.

Overseas, he extended his protection to every man in his squad. Fearful for the safety of his men during their first mission into combat, he dismissed the slim patrol of which he was in charge and himself became a casualty, but not before he had completed his mission. For his action, he was awarded the Bronze Star.

During the period of his basic training in the mountain country of North Carolina, Monty had met a Southern school teacher named Ann, and had married her. Upon his discharge, he returned to Ann and his two children and obtained a position as vocational guidance director at Brevard Junior College.

When he wasn't working, Monty attended classes at Western Carolina College, a small but well-regarded teachers' college in Cullowhee, North Carolina. One of his teachers, Professor W. B. Harrill, recalls with obvious satisfaction that "Monty was a young man who did not subscribe to what I call the regurgitation process. That's the process whereby a professor reads some passage from a highly esteemed book, jots down the essence of what he's read in his notebook and passes it along to his students. They, in turn, jot it down in their notebooks, and eventually regurgitate the material without polluting their response in any way with their own thinking. Well, Monty never did this. He questioned everything, which is what I think a real teacher has to do."

Monty became a teacher long before he received his diploma. Armed with only a provisional teaching certificate, he was appointed teaching principal at the Penrose School, a three-room schoolhouse in the mountain town of Little River, North Carolina. This was a region rich in illiteracy, inbreeding and home-brewed "likker." His backwoods boys and girls were poorly fed, poorly disciplined and poorly motivated for education. He did so well in winning over these "ignorant" youngsters that their fathers became fearful that he would woo them away to the big cities. Instead of appeasing these mountain folk, he tried to change their way of thinking and, as a result, found himself being run out of town. In a gesture of contempt, they had blown up the outhouse behind his home. Fearful for the safety of his family, Monty packed up and left Little River.

But his ability with the "socially disadvantaged," the "under-achiever" and the "educably retarded"—all terms that characterized the student body at the Penrose School—brought him to the attention of a man who ran a summer camp in North Carolina and a private school for "slow" children in Florida.

Monty accepted a teaching job at the school and moved his family to Miami, but within a year he became disenchanted. "I guess I didn't like working under somebody else," he admits. "But I also didn't like hearing that a child who just couldn't grasp things was unteachable. I just didn't see things that way. I don't think that this man really loved children. So I quit. But in the year I'd been there, I learned a lot. I learned what *not* to do with troubled kids."

During his brief tenure, Monty met Dr. Douglas A. Muncie, an osteopath who specialized in hearing defects. He worked in his free time with the doctor's young patients who, because of

their hearing disabilities, had developed emotional problems.
Dr. Muncie was ostracized by some of his colleagues for attempting to restore hearing by an unapproved bloodless operation
which he called "finger surgery." It consisted of reconstructing
the Eustachian tubes by means of simply pushing the index
finger through the mouth into the prolapsed tubes.

Monty was not bothered by the criticism which surrounded
this controversial practitioner. "What did I care about how he
got results?" Monty says with a shrug. "All I cared about was
that he did get results. He had kids who needed to be taught,
and I was a teacher."

Some of these youngsters had never heard before. Now they
could hear but could not understand what they heard and were
frightened of the "noises." Using a tape recorder donated by
the singer Rudy Vallee, Monty developed a method of auditory
perception that would free the children from reliance on lip-
reading and would render sounds both welcome and intelligible.

It was a long, slow process, but with each new success, Monty
experienced a rare feeling of satisfaction. The more difficult the
child, the more devoted he became. In other words, the emotional
disturbance that alienated the child from society had the effect
of putting Monty more in tune with the child.

He began to look about him, to check out the facilities available for severely disturbed children in Dade County. "I was
amazed to find that the public schools were full of kids who
couldn't get along in class," he recalls, in a voice heavy with
emotion. "Some were so sick that their parents chained them to
the bed to keep them out of trouble. If they were lucky enough
to be psychotic, they might be admitted to a state mental institution, but if their IQ was over seventy, they couldn't make it.
Even if they were admitted, chances were they'd wind up with
nothing more than custodial care. The places for retarded kids
had waiting lists a mile long and they wouldn't take a child who
was too difficult. The kids had to become social menaces before
any corrective action was taken and, once they wound up in a
state training school—that's a fancy name for reform school—
there wasn't much hope for them. I found that there were more
facilities for evaluating a child than for treating a child. As for

private psychiatrists, what good are a few hours a week of therapy for a kid who has to go back home to a family that doesn't want him or doesn't understand him? Some of these poor kids wound up in boarding homes out in the swamps where they were put away in wooden cages with bars that reach from the floor to the ceiling and where they received no therapy of any kind. In some instances, their hands were tied together behind their backs to keep them from chewing on their own flesh!"

Monty was convinced that these wasted remnants of human life could have been salvaged if there had been some help before their illness had become acute. To him, no child, however damaged, was expendable.

He made up his mind to start his own school and do things his own way. Even as he recalls the decision now, a sense of urgency enters his voice. "I knew I was a nobody, not even a qualified teacher except by experience," he says forthrightly, "but these kids can't wait for the best teachers to come along, to graduate college and get some basic training in the field. The way I see it, emotional disturbance is an emergency, no different from a burst appendix, a broken leg or a heart attack. You have to treat it right away or else it gets worse and spreads to other kids in the family. Sick kids like this don't need fancy facilities and a lot of them don't need psychiatrists; even the psychiatrists admit that. They need teachers, understanding human beings. That's how I felt then and that's how I feel now. Something has to be done for these kids right away and somebody has to do it. I felt that I could. At least, I sure as hell was going to try."

His convictions notwithstanding, Montanari's decision was not purely an emotional one. He carefully weighed his chances for success and discovered that he had a lot of things going for him in Hialeah: the lowest property-tax rate in the nation, year-round warm weather and ample community recreational and mental-health facilities.

Nevertheless, his wife, Ann, who taught normal children, did not completely share his enthusiasm. "I told him I didn't think it was good for anybody's mental health to deal with one kind of child all the time," she recalls. "You look at all the doctors and nurses in your psychotic wards and you can't tell the difference between the patients and the doctors. But Monty didn't agree and didn't even answer me."

Monty had rented an old-fashioned two-story frame house for his family in a lovely residential area known as Deer Park, in the heart of Hialeah. The house was run down, all but buried under a heavy overgrowth of bougainvillea vines, gnarled old eucalyptus trees and white hibiscus shrubs. But the yard surrounding it was huge, encompassing three city lots, and included four bungalow-size greyhound kennels. The property had deteriorated to the point where it had become an eyesore, and the landlord was only too glad to sell it for a down payment of four thousand dollars and a mere 4-percent interest on the mortgage.

Monty invited his parents down from Winchendon and talked his father into lending him four thousand dollars. At first reluctant to part with his savings, his father finally relented, explaining in his self-taught English, "I figger that my boy, he don' make much money at this here teachin', but at least he gotter use his head."

Reliance on brains, rather than on brawn, meant a great deal to Monty's father. But brawn was necessary in the beginning. During the first few weeks, Monty and his father worked from sunup to sundown, clearing away the excess of twisting vines and knee-high shrubbery. They trimmed the grass, patched the screens and mended the loose boards. They painted the whole house, inside and out, and fixed up the greyhound kennels with old chairs and discarded school desks to give them the appearance of classrooms.

In February, 1952, Monty opened a day school for disturbed children in his own home, raising them along with his own children. Gary was then four, and Cissy three. Dr. Muncie helped him to get started by referring to him young patients whose hearing problems had led to emotional problems.

The first child admitted to the school was a nine-year-old girl, a congenital syphilitic who was almost totally deaf, nearly blind from cataracts, and suffering from a cardiac condition. Her name was Sylvia and she was homely, ungainly and, as a result of her many misfortunes, severely disturbed emotionally. She shrieked, struck out, and wept uncontrollably when she wasn't behaving aggressively. Her parents had walked out on her when she was only an infant and she had been raised by an aunt and uncle who had no other children and regarded her as their own daughter.

The uncle, a commercial fisherman, was barely able to make a living and could not afford to pay Monty the hundred-dollar-a-month tuition, so Monty agreed to accept fish in payment. Each morning, Sylvia's uncle would bring her to Monty's home, and when he picked her up late in the afternoon, he would leave a catch of fresh fish as compensation.

Dr. Muncie treated Sylvia's hearing problem and succeeded in increasing her hearing level from 10 to 66 percent. Monty then took over and taught her to distinguish words. Her rapid progress led him to believe that Sylvia's intelligence had been very underrated and that her physical disabilities were responsible for her emotional difficulties.

He went to the Hialeah Lions Club and persuaded the membership to finance eye surgery for the girl. He secured the services of a leading eye specialist to remove the cataracts. The operation was successful.

He then went to Variety Children's Hospital and begged for a doctor to volunteer his services for an open-heart operation. He shamed a doctor into performing the operation and this, too, proved eminently successful. Now Sylvia no longer had to lie in bed half the day. She could see and hear and could get around as well as any other child.

To make her more amenable to both emotional and social re-education, he cut her hair, bought her some new clothes and, in every way possible, removed the stigma of being different. Monty kept Sylvia occupied. She swept the floor, made the beds, washed and cooked. He played music on the radio to reinforce her familiarity with sounds other than talk. In short, he transformed her from an ugly misfit with nothing to live for into an attractive, healthy, lively child who became eager to deal with life on its own terms. And only after she had ceased to rage, to cry, to spit, did he endeavor to confront her with the rudiments of formal education.

"She was a human being," he says, "and that's all I cared about. I knew she'd never become the valedictorian of her class, but I also knew that she would be able to cope with life. She could make her own way, you see, that was the important thing."

Word of his success with Sylvia got around but it wasn't enough to overcome objections to his assuming the functions of a professional without the credentials. The situation remained precarious. Lacking cash, credentials and connections, Monty redoubled his efforts to prove his abilities with rejected youngsters.

He placed small advertisements in the local newspapers for "difficult children with no place to go," but received few replies. He made the rounds of neighborhood doctors, psychologists, psychiatrists and social agencies, pleading for "castoffs," those children who were so terribly disturbed that nobody wanted to work with them because they seemed to be beyond help. Door after door was slammed in his face because of his lack of qualifications, but he persevered. Like a good salesman he returned again and again with a smile on his face. His behavior was, in a way, a replay of his boyhood, when, slapped across the mouth by his mother, he would go out one door only to return, smiling, by another.

His tenacity was rewarded. Lacking patience with Monty as well as with the children who seemed to be "unmotivated for therapy," a number of doctors and agencies surrendered one child, then another, and another, simply because there was no other place to send them.

Aware that he had to prove himself, Monty devoted himself passionately to these children for the eight hours that they remained in his charge, and sent them back to the referring doctors at frequent intervals for reevaluation.

To these youngsters, he became a father substitute. He accepted their abnormal behavior and allowed them to act out their frustrations. The child who demanded food was fed as much as he wanted until he stopped eating of his own accord. The child who wanted to smash windows was permitted to do so—safely, with a baseball bat—until he tired of the pastime. The child who could not control his impulse to cut himself with a knife was handed a knife and told, "Go ahead," then carefully observed while he took a superficial nick of flesh, and tossed the knife aside.

"You have to be diagnostic," Monty explains. "You have to know the child you're dealing with. You can't be overprotective with these kids because that will only increase their dependency. But you can't have a kid who threatens to hang himself climb up a tree and try it with a crowd around, because then he's liable to do it."

He gave his children attention, affection and encouragement. He toilet-trained them and brought them into contact with his own and other children when they began to show a willingness to abandon their hostilities or emerge from their shells. He first taught them how to live on an elemental level and then taught them their ABC's.

"I remember I had a little girl of six who couldn't put on her panties except inside out," he says by way of demonstrating his approach to such children. "So I got some red thread and sewed some red buttons on the front. Then I didn't have to tell her, 'Honey, you didn't do it right.' She knew the right way, when the red buttons were in front, and that kind of success means a lot to such a child."

In or out of the classroom, he made every learning experience therapeutic and came up with his own way of doing things. The little boy who stole as a matter of course was given a few pennies and taken to the local dime store to buy a toy for himself. Much was made of the transaction and the little boy became entranced by the process. He was given simple tasks—shining shoes, putting books away, cleaning the table after lunch—and rewarded in small change for his efforts. He was then taken to the store to exchange his money for inexpensive playthings. The more work he did, the greater was his remuneration and the better the toys he could purchase. When this fundamental truth penetrated his deepest feelings, he no longer had the need to steal. He had learned the meaning of pride in accomplishment along with elementary economics.

As Monty taught, he himself learned. He learned that some children needed to be made anxious in order to take interest in their young lives. The autistic child—frozen, withdrawn, asocial —fell into this category. He found that there were times when he had to jar such a child from his placidity with a slap, a shout or the sudden withdrawal of some expected pleasure. The shock of such treatment served to bend the child to the needs of his or her environment and to swing the numb youngster back to reality.

"This kind of thing had to be done at the right time, the precise moment when it was the most effective," says Monty, wagging a finger to emphasize his words. "I learned pretty fast that every child, even every autistic child, is different and must be handled according to his individual needs. Sometimes they needed appeasing more than they needed being shocked, and all of them needed tenderness. I've never found a set of rules that would apply to all kids at all times. You have to study each one individually. It takes time. You can't be in a hurry."

Generally, he found that lectures, beatings and admonitions to conform were futile in reeducating emotionally disturbed children. He dealt out rewards and punishments in much the same manner as an animal trainer who tries to domesticate and educate a tiger, a monkey or a seal, but Monty went farther because he was dealing with children, not animals. He had to struggle to reach into the mind and soul of a child in order to make the reconditioning process permanent and meaningful.

For almost three years, he lived from hand to mouth, attending the University of Miami several evenings a week to earn his State Teaching Certificate and take special courses in education and psychology. During the summer, when his day pupils returned to their families, he continued his studies at Western Carolina College and, in 1955, received his BS in education.

"It didn't mean a damn thing to me," he says with an impatient wave of his hand, "but it seemed to mean a lot to the people I had to get along with."

Professor Harrill, who knows him well, recalls, "When Monty was studying during the summer, he sometimes brought along a few highly disturbed young fellows with whom he worked very closely, while augmenting his income with the few dollars their families paid him. Many nights I looked out my window and saw Monty chasing these boys across the campus when they tried to run off. It all struck me as so hopeless. I could see no way out for him in such an undertaking but it was plain that he felt differently."

What was hopeless to Professor Harrill was challenging to Montanari. By the time he received his diploma, he was convinced that the only answer to the problems of intensely disturbed children lay in "residential treatment geared to reeducation" and, upon his return to Hialeah, applied for a zoning permit to allow him to take in residential students.

He decided to try working with a different kind of child than he had dealt with in the past and found such an opportunity when the juvenile court entrusted to his care a fierce little eight-year-old named Charlie, but better known to those acquainted with him as "Little Capone."

III

Young Charlie Hummert arrived at the Clinical School accompanied by his father, a dour, slow-witted man, and a probation officer from the juvenile court. The boy's behavior was exemplary, quite unlike what Monty expected after studying the dossier forwarded to him by the authorities.

"The way Charlie came in here," recalls Monty with a wry grin, "nobody would believe he was a little terror. He kept saying 'Yes, sir' very politely to his daddy and the probation officer, even to me. Oh, God, he had me fooled. He was a skinny little fellow with a pasty face and I remember thinking that the Florida sunshine would do him good. I'd agreed to take him on a trial basis for three months because everybody in Ohio had given up on him—the schools, the social agencies, even the courts. Well, after one look at Charlie, I figured everybody had him wrong, that he was going to be real easy and I'd have him back home in no time. But I found out pretty fast how wrong I was."

No sooner had Mr. Hummert and the probation officer driven off, than a dramatic change came over the boy. Suddenly, he was no longer the innocent, trusting, well-mannered child. Alone with Monty in his small office, the boy's body stiffened. He seemed to grow inches taller. His eyes narrowed, his lips tightened and his attitude changed swiftly from one of innocence to belligerence. He swaggered boldly up to Monty, seated behind an old school desk, spread his hands across the desk and leaned over it menacingly.

"If I had a knife," he said, "I'd kill you."

Thinking back to the incident, Monty admits, "It would be an understatement to say he caught me off guard. But I tried not to let on. I just sat there, not saying anything, playing for time. Then I began to see that he was testing me. This was our first conflict. I knew I had to win because he'd never trust me unless I came out on top. So I had no choice. I had to take a chance on the boy. I reached into my desk drawer, took out a letter opener and shoved it across the desk to Charlie, without saying a word. Well, that kid was so surprised he didn't know what to do. He stared at the letter opener, then he stared at me. His face began to twitch and he sat down in the little chair in front of the desk and started to cry. He cried just like a baby. I let him go on for a while and then I said to him, 'Charlie, why'd you want to use a knife on me?' He kept on crying, then looked away from me and said, 'Don't ask me why I act this way, it's my own business whatever I do.' So I said, 'OK, Charlie.' Then I went over and put my arm around him, and said, 'Come on, let's take a walk around and I'll show you the place.' "

Once outside, Charlie's personality altered again. Another boy, swinging from an old tire hung from the branch of a mango tree, pointed a finger at him and, for no apparent reason, began to laugh. Instantly, Charlie tore himself from Monty and went for the boy. He dragged him off the makeshift swing, threw him to the ground, and sitting astride him, shook him violently.

Monty raced over to the shrieking boy, pulled Charlie away and said, "Settle down, son, settle down."

Charlie put his head down shamefacedly and said he was sorry. He shook hands with the boy and asked Monty if he could stay out in the yard to play by himself. Monty agreed.

Before a half hour elapsed, Charlie had threatened to beat up every child in the school and had chalked vulgar four-letter words across the side of the house.

Then, spotting a small bird that had alighted on the grass, Charlie decided to give a further demonstration of his "toughness." With remarkable swiftness, he trapped the trembling bird.

Grinning with satisfaction, he looked around to be sure that everyone's eyes were on him. And, with the same quick agility he had shown in capturing the bird, he bit off its head and spit it out into the grass, flinging the carcass after it. A triumphant smile lit up his face as he smeared away the thin line of blood on his chin. Watching him, spellbound, two children retched, several cheered and the rest just stared, unable to react.

"He showed no sign of remorse at the time," Montanari comments, "and this seemed to confirm the diagnosis of Charlie as a sociopath or psychopath, somebody who doesn't give a damn about the rest of society. But I had the feeling that this was a boy who didn't give a damn about *himself* and did the crazy things he did because he was looking for punishment. I mean, if he really didn't have a conscience, he would've knifed me when I offered him the chance. He wouldn't have broken down and cried. So I didn't think he was really a delinquent or had the kind of character disorder you can't do much about. To me, he was just an angry little kid, much angrier than any kid I'd ever known before, and that's why I wanted to work with him. At the time, my wife helped to keep me going by teaching school. I knew that if I could show results with a boy as sick as Charlie, I might get support from the professionals who sneered at me and be able to make out on my own."

So little Charlie Hummert became a test of strength to Montanari. Others had tried and failed. There was even disagreement over Charlie's basic problem and treatment. According to the juvenile-court records, the child-guidance center which had subjected the boy to a battery of psychological tests diagnosed him as suffering from "a sociopathic personality disturbance with antisocial reaction," and advised that "it is doubtful if he would be amenable to psychotherapy, but is in need of long-term care in a closed school where firm, consistent and patient controls can be applied."

An equally intensive appraisal by a juvenile diagnostic center advised the same juvenile-court judge that Charlie suffered from "an adjustment reaction to childhood with some evidence of being emotionally disturbed," and recommended "treatment on an out-patient basis while remaining in the family setting."

To resolve these conflicting opinions, the court psychologist put Charlie through still more tests and interviews, finally concluding that he suffered from "a personality-trait disturbance due to faulty emotional development," and advised that "even temporary return home at this time would be contraindicated." The court psychologist tabbed Charlie's need for care "urgent," and suggested, with obvious reluctance, that "if the county does not have funds for placement in a residential treatment center, commitment to the Boys' Industrial School"—reform school— "would appear to be the only acknowledgedly poor alternative."

Montanari, in his outspoken way, refers to this clash of professional opinion as "nomenclature masturbation," and he explains his feelings with an impatient gesture of his hand. "They go over this boy bit by bit, testing him and retesting him, and then they still can't agree on what's wrong with him or what to do to help the child. I know they mean well, I know they're trying to do what's best for the child, but they just keep playing with themselves intellectually. The kid sits around and nobody does anything for him. While they bicker back and forth, he gets worse and worse waiting for something to happen. But nothing ever does. He just goes on waiting, getting worse and worse."

True to form, no local facilities were available for Charlie in his home town in Ohio. There were insufficient funds for residential care elsewhere and, even if funds had been available, no residential-treatment center wanted Charlie. Since the court had ruled against his remaining at home and receiving psychotherapy on an out-patient basis, the only alternative seemed to be reform school, where it was unlikely he would recover sufficiently to return to society. It would be the end of the road.

But fortunately for Charlie, a social worker had become familiar with Montanari's setup and, once all other possibilities had been exhausted, Monty was contacted. As usual, he was the last resort. It was true to the pattern of Monty's development in the field. Monty accepted the boy for residential care at the same rate he charged for day care—one hundred dollars a month —and said that if he felt he could help Charlie, he would go out and try to raise additional funds himself.

What sort of boy was this who had reached such a dead end at the early age of eight? What was there, in his genes or in his environment, that had turned him into a little pariah? What in Charlie's young life had conspired to make him an outcast from the human race?

Little Charlie Hummert had known the sound and fury of violence almost from the day of his birth. Two brothers and two sisters had preceded him into the world. He had what is known as a "whole family." His father worked hard, as a machinist, but was forced to augment his income with odd jobs during weekends and evening hours. Overworked and overburdened, Mr. Hummert took out his frustrations on his family. He was quick of temper, punitive and inconsiderate. Mrs. Hummert, on the other hand, was mild-mannered, almost meek. Patiently she absorbed both the emotional and the physical beatings which her husband administered. Somehow, Charlie's brothers and sisters were able to withstand the inconsistencies in parental behavior. Not Charlie. Perhaps he was born too late. Or perhaps, as one psychologist suggested, he was simply "more sensitive."

But neither parent had the time, intelligence or inclination to ponder the subtleties of young Charlie's personality. The father remained harsh, the mother ineffectual and the siblings hostile. They showed no understanding. They merely smiled or scowled, depending on their mood, when Charlie, at the age of two, displayed interest in peeking under women's dresses; at the age of three, drowned the family cat; at the age of four, made it necessary for the family to get rid of their dog because he took the dog's penis into his mouth; and at the age of five, set his first fire in the backyard and almost burned the house down.

By the time Charlie entered public school, he had become blatantly destructive, disruptive and defiant. The school psychologist must have spent some time investigating the boy's background and family situation because he wrote in his record: "This is a pretty impossible home situation for a boy to live in."

But the father was too strong and the mother too weak to remedy the situation. The curious thing was that each, in their own way, loved Charlie, but neither could adequately convey that love. For they did not truly love one another and, somehow, Charlie seemed to sense this. A social worker who looked in on the family at the suggestion of the school psychologist reported: "The mother admits that the marriage relationship has been poor but feels divorce is out of the question for the children's sake."

It is an old story, but the irony of it all escaped Charlie's parents. The awareness of what was happening to their son eluded them because of their own emotional instability.

Mr. Hummert tried to beat Charlie into submissiveness. "Dad makes me read to him," the boy told a social worker, "and if I don't know a word, he counts to three, then slaps me in the face."

When Charlie did poorly in a spelling test at school, he was spanked hard ten times for every word that he had misspelled. In the compositions he was called upon to write in public school, he did not refer to such treatment by his father, but he did frequently write such sentences as "I wish Mom and Dad would be happy so they wouldn't fight all the time." Plainly, the lack of love in his home was upsetting to Charlie.

In first grade, Charlie stole a five-dollar bill from his teacher's pocketbook. In second grade, Charlie joined some older boys who broke into a neighborhood store to steal a BB gun. In third grade, Charlie sampled a cigarette one night when exploring a nearby grain mill, tossed it aside and burned down the mill. Not long after, he took a walk to the railroad tracks outside of town and, finding a heavy steel bar lying nearby, dragged it to the tracks. He placed it across the tracks, then stood by waiting excitedly for a train to come by and be derailed. Fortunately for the passengers and crew, the obstruction was spotted by a watchman and removed before a disaster could occur.

Each time Charlie was confronted and accused of wrongdoing, he readily admitted to having committed the "prank." His reason for doing so was nearly always the same: "I got mad because I didn't get my own way at home."

The family pastor talked with the Hummerts and urged them to confer with a social worker at the local family-service agency. They agreed. They talked with the social worker many times but seemed unable to profit from the guidance. Mr. Hummert continued to try to "beat some sense" into Charlie and, if Mrs. Hummert dared protest, he would shout at her and slap her. This fed Charlie's hostility and need to strike back. The rebellion began to take the form of fire-setting, and Charlie is on record as saying, "Every time my ma or I got beat, I went out and set a fire."

As a result, he was in and out of detention homes, spending more time there than in school. His attempt to derail the train brought the local chief of police and several police officers into the Hummert home. The police record of the incident reads: "We were met at the front door by the boy's father and were advised that we would have to come inside to talk to the boy since he was not able to leave the house. Upon entering the living room, we found the boy sitting in a straight-backed chair with a one-half-inch manila hemp rope tied to his left ankle. The rope measured approximately thirty-two feet in length. The other end of the rope was tied to a water pipe in another room. The father advised us that the boy was being punished for breaking the law."

When questioned about the severity of his discipline, Mr. Hummert was unable to explain why he was so abusive toward Charlie other than to say that he wanted him to be a "good boy." Quite probably, for similar reasons, he did not object to the boy's being removed from the home and sent to Montanari's for treatment.

"Charlie had been subjected to a lot of violence in his conditioning," points out Monty. "Violence had penetrated the sanctity of the home, which should have been a refuge from the turmoil and hostility of the outside world, but it wasn't. He never had the kind of security which was his right as a little boy. But despite everything, Charlie had a lot going for him. Somehow, enough love seemed to have got through to make him want to get well and to go back home. Now, this is the motivation that I look for, the desire of a child to return home. This gives me an edge, something to work with. Charlie's mama was wishy-washy but she was kind to him and that helped him a lot. His daddy was a brute and that didn't help, but he was strong and very masculine and Charlie identified with him. So he didn't have a sex problem. He was just trying to be a brute like his old man. He may have hated him, but he loved him, too, because there were lots of things they enjoyed doing together, like fishing and hunting. Charlie tried to control situations the way his daddy did, by being brutal, you see, or else he'd just go to pieces. It's the kind of background that's typical of many delinquents today. Charlie was lucky in that he was still very young and his basic character was still flexible."

Jack Blanton, chief probation officer of Dade County Juvenile Court, is an underpaid, overworked man who deals with kids like Charlie Hummert every day. His job has made him somewhat cynical but not hopeless, because he loves children, seeks out the best in them and, literally, fights City Hall to rehabilitate them. Monty had him meet Charlie and he says, "I will never forget that boy. I don't know who else would take him but Monty. The youngsters who come to my attention have been through everybody's front room. They've been to the principal, the dean, the recreation director, the preacher, the coach, the private psychiatrist, they've been the whole route. By the time they get to us, very few people are interested in working with them because they're too disturbed. Like an eleven-year-old boy I have on my hands right now. The mental hospital won't take him, we don't want to put him in jail, and he can't go home. So what's left? If he doesn't get help fast, he's liable to kill somebody someday. There's no door open to him in the whole state except at Montanari's and I don't think the other states are much better off. This is a shame, but it's a fact."

Montanari desperately wanted to reclaim Charlie Hummert for society, to return him to his home and to public school. But the Clinical School was still a one-man operation. Except for a part-time maid who came by for a few hours each day to put things in order, Monty was doing everything from preparing breakfast to tucking the children into bed. Plainly, he needed help, and shortly before Charlie arrived, he engaged another teacher, Mrs. Ruth Griffin, who today is his assistant director.

A diploma from a southern junior college and scattered experience as a substitute teacher were her only academic qualifications. More important, to Montanari, was the fact that she had raised three children of her own and showed great enthusiasm for dealing with the difficult youngsters attending his school.

"I was impressed," says Monty, "not by her credentials, but by her attitude and personality. I felt that she liked kids, that she really did, and that she could reach out to my kids."

Ruth Griffin is a tall, slim, fragile-looking woman with a handsome touch of gray in her neatly combed hair, and appears to be extremely calm and self-possessed. She combines the soft manner of a Southern gentlewoman, the firmness of a schoolteacher and the effortless smile of a welcome guest at a family reunion.

"I just didn't know what to make of Monty when I first came here," she recalls. "He kept leading me from one classroom to another, kept moving me from one group of children to another. I'd work with the boys, then he'd move me over to the girls. I'd work with children who were withdrawn, then he'd move me over to those who acted out. And finally I said to him, 'Golly, can't I do anything right around here? Why do you keep moving me around all the time?' And he laughed, saying, 'You're doing just fine. But I want to give you some experience working with all kinds of kids, that's all.' And to this day, that's how he tests people. He puts them in one spot after another to see how they handle the situation. I guess you might say he gives them enough rope to hang themselves. If they don't, he keeps them on."

But despite Ruth Griffin's ability to survive Montanari's intensive testing of her flexibility, she found herself shocked by Charlie Hummert. "He was a little devil," she remembers. "He gave orders to everyone. His favorite expression was, 'The master has spoken, do what he says.' And I just couldn't hit it off with him because we didn't seem to be able to warm up to one another."

Her inability to communicate with Charlie didn't faze Monty. "It was a personality clash, that's all," he says. "This particular child and this particular adult just didn't go together. And I told Mrs. Griffin, 'Nobody can love *all* children. So if you can't get along with Charlie, leave him alone. He'll appeal to someone else.' And the strangest thing is that Charlie got along real well with Ruth's husband, Jim, who had come to work for me, doing occupational therapy and taking the kids on trips into town, to the public swimming pool, the movies and the library. Aside from myself, Jim became Charlie's best friend."

Jim Griffin is a husky, no-nonsense sort of man, and may have reminded Charlie of his own father. But Jim was more flexible, more charitable, and so was able to reach deeper into the heart of the boy. Jim had a small boat and Monty allowed Charlie to work on the boat when his behavior merited such treats.

"Many times Charlie merely played at being a good boy so he would be allowed on Jim's boat," admits Monty. "Right afterward, he was just as bad as ever. Some people accused me of using 'emotional blackmail,' of forcing Charlie to behave just to get a reward. But that didn't bother me. It's my feeling that if a child can learn to act positively enough times and sustain that good behavior for a while, then you are altering his personality. The child comes to realize that while poor behavior may not bring punishment, it won't bring rewards. This is what I had to get through to this boy because he was so hard to handle. Very rough. Sometimes he became so wild I felt that if I didn't hold him together, he'd just fly apart."

For the first few weeks, Charlie's behavior was so unpredictable, so far-out, that he had to be watched closely at all times. He broke windows, smashed lamps, dishes and toys. In class, he used the foulest language imaginable. He stole money from Monty's desk, from Mrs. Griffin's handbag and from the pockets of visitors who left their jackets in Monty's office. He tried to run away many times. Matches were withheld from him because he would use them to start brush fires in the yard at the slightest provocation. When asked what he would like most for his birthday, he answered, "Three sticks of dynamite to blow up the school."

Despite Charlie's misbehavior, Monty refused to set too many limits on the boy. "I was afraid to restrict him too much," he says. "I didn't want to overdiscipline him because I was concerned that if I cut off all opportunities for negative behavior, he would only get worse."

Ruth Griffin tells how Monty cautioned her not to fight back with Charlie. "The more you fight back," he wrote in a memo, "the more strength Charlie will get to keep up the fight."

When Charlie broke windows, he had to earn the cost of replacement by performing simple chores such as sweeping the floor of his room or mowing the lawn. Jim Griffin converted the installation of new panes of glass into occupational therapy for other boys.

When Charlie slapped himself in the face and accused someone else of striking him, his chicanery was greeted with a shrug of the shoulders. "He was looking for punishment," explains Monty, "because this is what he was used to and he knew that *we* knew what he was up to. It's common for disturbed children to seek out punishment and you have to know when to punish and when not to. If you punish a child just because he wants it, you won't cure his bad behavior. You'll only make it easier for him to go on misbehaving. I punished Charlie only when he was hurting another child, and it had to be done at the right moment."

Montanari is no advocate of corporal punishment but he thinks there are other forms of punishment that can be even more damaging and of more permanent effect: slurs and sarcasm, disrespect for the child's rights, subtle rejection such as might be evidenced by continual scowling disapproval, and correcting the child in front of other youngsters. He points out that it is not uncommon, when a little dog expresses fear, for the dog's master to soothe the animal, but when a little boy expresses fear, the same "master" might belittle the child as a "namby-pamby," or try to "whip the fear out of him."

On the other hand, Montanari does not completely disavow the need for all corporal punishment. "I can't let one of my kids get away with hurting another," he says. "When Charlie tried to stab another boy with a pencil, I spanked him. But I'd caught him in the act. There was an element of surprise in my spanking him. It was unexpected, you see, and I think that punishment has to be unexpected if it is to be effective in helping to recondition the child to more acceptable behavior. I know for a fact that most residential centers often use corporal punishment on their kids but they call it 'disciplinary action.' Now, that's just a euphemism. I prefer to call a spade a spade."

Charlie was crafty. He liked to emulate well-known gangsters and organized some of the other boys into a gang, to make it easier for him to manipulate the rest of the children as well as the adults around him. He would sometimes get out from behind his desk in class, sweep books and papers off the desks around him and announce, "Me and my boys ain't goin' to stay in class today!"

Such behavior led to his being nicknamed "Little Capone" and the children whom he tried to victimize referred to him by that epithet more often than by his true name. His arrogance, however, annoyed even those boys who had joined his "gang" and they began to withdraw from him, refusing to talk to him, and banded together with the other children to declare a "Hate Charlie Hummert Week."

Monty recalls how this upset Charlie. "There is a time to talk and a time not to talk when you're dealing with disturbed kids," Monty says, "and I felt that now was a time to talk. I took Charlie aside and told him, 'If you have to do these things, to pick on other kids and raise hell the way you do, it's OK with me, Charlie. But if you want to straighten up, I can help you. I can help you act so that the other kids will like you better and so will your mama and daddy. You'll be able to go home a lot sooner. It's all up to you.' Well, he listened but I wasn't sure that I was getting through. I even said to him, 'Charlie, if you want to fight, fight with me, not with the other kids.' But it was hard to fathom what Charlie was going to do next. With a boy as sick as this, there were no pat answers. You had to sway with the hurricane and decide how to handle each situation as it came along. It was going to take time."

During this trying period, an old friend of Montanari's, Dr. Benjamin A. Stevens, the supervisor of schools in Transylvania County, North Carolina, visited the Clinical School. Startled and deeply moved by Charlie and the other children he came into contact with, he wrote a report of his visit:

The Montanari Clinical School has its system, its routine and ordered procedures, but at first you lose this sense of there being an organized operating plan. You see nothing but individual children and the pathetic inadequacies of these children command your whole attention and tear at your heart. You stand in a state of bafflement and wonder how any order can come out of such a chaos of addled personalities. Here is Larry, babbling over and over, 'Mama come? Mama come?' Over there is Anita, who periodically attempts to choke herself blue in the face with a shoelace. And here comes Little Capone offering to tie a tight knot around Anita's neck. You see Monty racing from one supposedly hopeless situation to another. Then, gradually, the odd-shaped pieces of personality begin to fit into a whole cloth and you begin to see the school in a different light. With a feeling short of amazement, you are struck by the realization that there is, after all, a routine, a variety of techniques, a method to all this madness. You may continue to wonder how Larry and Anita and Little Capone will ever achieve success at anything, even the simplest tasks, but you can't help but notice that they are learning, actually getting somewhere, making new lives for themselves.

Dr. Stevens passed along one important suggestion to Montanari before he returned home. "In my experience," he told him, "I've found that any child, emotionally disturbed or not, must be given an opportunity to achieve success. With success comes learning. But he has to experience that success and feel it. It's like someone trying to develop marksmanship with a rifle. He shoots at the target, but if he doesn't see where the bullet lands, he can't improve. He needs that satisfaction of seeing that he hit his mark in order to get the urge to shoot again."

This observation made a strong impression on Montanari and he used this technique on Charlie Hummert. While Charlie continued to write out his spelling lesson by printing his letters backward, presumably to attract attention or perhaps punishment, Monty had him do them over, not reprimanding him but simply explaining that the boy could advance himself by doing his lessons correctly. After a week of such treatment, Charlie began to spell in more orthodox fashion and Monty rewarded him immediately with a smile of pleasure and advancement to a higher grade, taking pains to point out the reason for such advancement.

It took many months before Charlie showed signs of change in his overall personality. The first clue was his transfer of hostility from others to himself. He ceased his attacks on his playmates and took to biting his toenails ferociously before going to bed. The other children laughed at him and Monty said to Charlie, "They're laughing because they don't bite their toenails. That's why they think it's funny. You can go on and bite them all you want. But I can't promise to make them stop laughing. You're the only one who can stop them, Charlie, you're in the driver's seat. Maybe you can switch over to biting your fingernails instead. Lots of kids do that."

A few days after he'd planted the thought in Charlie's mind, the boy did switch to biting his fingernails. Monty made a big thing of this. "I couldn't be casual about this with a boy like Charlie," he explains. "It was a big step for him."

The better part of a year went by and Mr. and Mrs. Hummert wrote letters to Charlie telling him how much they missed him. Their letters whetted Charlie's impatience to return home and he began to complain to anyone who would listen, "This place ain't no fuckin' good and nobody here is no fuckin' good. I hate this fuckin' place and want to go home."

His resort to vulgarity was his way of expressing his displeasure as well as his confusion. He was protesting too much, for his behavior was far better than his outbursts indicated. He had progressed to the point where verbal vulgarity had become his chief means of rebellion.

But his parents were also putting pressure on Montanari. They had moved to a farm in the country and there was opportunity for Charlie to fish and hunt. Typical of the many letters written to Monty by Mrs. Hummert is the following:

We love Charlie very much and try in many ways to show our love. His brothers and sisters miss him and need their brother to look up to and be proud of. Charlie will never do anything for the children to be ashamed of. For he has learned a great lesson. It has been hard for him and for us. Now that we have moved to new surroundings, it will be good for all of us. There is a stream nearby where a boy could go fishing with his dad. Give us our chance with our boy. Please, Mr. Montanari. We love him. We need him.

Monty squinted through the Ben Franklin spectacles atop his nose at the letter and carefully shoved it back into Charlie's file. "I guess I've read this letter a hundred times," he said, "and I never stop wondering how a parent can block out reality the way so many do. I mean, this boy was practically lost to society, set for jail or a mental institution. The whole neighborhood was up in arms about him, the police had to be called in, he'd been expelled from school, yet to Mama he's just an ordinary kid who's away from home for a while. She's sincere enough but she just doesn't seem to comprehend what her boy has been through. She and her husband keep writing how much they love him but they don't seem to realize that you can't tell a child you love him, that you have to show it."

Charlie was not yet ready to be discharged. He had improved a great deal, had learned to get along better with other children and, instead of beating them up when he became angry, had learned to accept the challenge of a fair fight, with either Monty or Jim Griffin refereeing the battle.

When Montanari had the boy reevaluated by a local psychologist, the report indicated "signs of healthy neuroticism": a fear of the dark, of new experiences with other children and of such fantasy objects as flying saucers. This was progress. In fact, the time had come when Charlie could be allowed to "run away," because his fear of the dark caused him to return soon after twilight.

As an additional check on the boy's progress, Montanari arranged for Charlie to be interviewed by a neighborhood child psychiatrist. The doctor recommended that Charlie be given at least three hours a week of psychotherapy, asserting that he seemed "amenable to treatment." This would require seventy-five dollars a week and no such funds were available.

"I was only getting one hundred dollars a month from the authorities," says Monty, "and this didn't even pay my expenses to keep the boy in residence. But I kept him because there was nothing else I could do, no place else for him to go, and I knew

I was getting somewhere with Charlie. Psychoanalysis, of course, was out for Charlie because with a boy like that, you don't go stirring up the ashes of the past. But I agreed with the psychiatrist that Charlie might profit from psychotherapy simply because his folks were so indifferent toward it themselves and were doing nothing to help themselves understand their son better. So Charlie needed to learn how to understand them. The only trouble was, I didn't have the money to pay for a doctor."

With all due respect to the qualified professionals in the field, it is nevertheless a sad commentary on the commercialism that has penetrated their practice to note that Montanari could obtain no qualified practitioner to donate his services to this child. Charlie, and other children, were in fact draining Monty's own slim savings. In a desperate move to call attention to the plight of these youngsters, Monty pleaded with the local press to visit his school and see the children for themselves, hopeful that they would be moved to write a story about his work and assist him in raising funds to care for children like Charlie.

The reporters did come. They met Charlie and wrote about him in their papers. Stories in the *Miami Herald* and other papers about "Little Capone" opened the way for Monty to meet with various civic groups and to solicit scholarships for children unable to pay their way.

At that particular moment, the Opti-Mrs. Club of Miami Beach, a service club of more than a hundred women interested in child welfare, had been knocking on the door of the Dade County Mental Health Association to ask if there were any disturbed youngsters whom they might assist. When they read about Charlie in their local papers, they immediately contacted Montanari and invited him to attend one of their luncheons.

Monty brought Charlie along with him and, in full view of the audience, the boy suddenly drew a thumbtack from his pocket and shoved it deeply into his knee, requiring a visit from a doctor.

"I don't really know why Charlie did such a thing," confesses Monty, "except that maybe he wanted to get attention for himself. But, in a way, I'm glad it happened, for Charlie's sake and for the sake of all the other kids that these women have helped. Because Charlie's action shocked these people and dramatized the need for funds."

Following the thumbtack incident, Monty told the Opti-Mrs.: "I intend to beat the bushes to raise money for this boy and for any other children who need my help. But to do a job for them, I need your help. Will you help me?"

Montanari's sincerity, his willingness to invite inspection of his school at any time and his easygoing manner charmed the members of the club. From that moment on, the Opti-Mrs. took a lively interest in the children at the Montanari School. With the help of such celebrities as Jimmy Durante, Danny Thomas and Buddy Hackett, they have since raised thousands of dollars in scholarship funds for more than a hundred indigent youngsters.

"We sponsor the children, not Monty," points out Mrs. Murray Sonnet, a past president of the Opti-Mrs. "We visit the children and can actually see their progress as they grow into useful little citizens. This gives us a very personal stake in their future."

Mrs. Seymour Silverman, formerly in charge of special projects for the group, adds, "We've raised funds for many worthy groups, but only Monty has produced. We're welcome at the school whenever we care to visit the children whose scholarships we've underwritten and it's a wonderful feeling to hear a child say, when you bring along a small gift of candy, 'You don't have to bring anything when you visit me, just come!' That's how hungry these youngsters are for affection."

The Opti-Mrs. made it possible for Charlie to receive an hour of psychotherapy a week. This was supplemented by weekly soul-searching conversations with Monty and an intensification of Charlie's relationship with Jim Griffin aboard Jim's boat, where the boy could find a physical outlet for his repressed feelings.

Some fifteen months after Charlie's arrival at the school, Montanari felt that he had done all he could for the boy and that he was ready to go home. Mr. and Mrs. Hummert had changed only superficially but Charlie had changed dramatically. He had come to grips with himself. He had made the grade.

His last letter to Monty, after returning home, reads: "Hi, Mr. Monty. I am finally getting time to write to you. I am getting along fine now. Are you getting along fine without me? I am going to public school and I enjoy it. It is fun to ride the bus and I have many new friends. I am real happy."

And to Charlie, Monty wrote: "I was very happy to hear from you and learn that you are getting along so well. I am very, very proud of you. Have fun, do your best at school and come visit me one of these days. I am sending you your savings-account book with a little surprise in it because you have been such a good boy." To the boy's savings, Montanari had added an additional fifty dollars from his own pocket.

This is the style of the man. It is indicative of the intense personal interest he takes in the children entrusted to him. By a very natural process that might be called "tender communication," he had been able to reach into the heart and soul of "Little Capone," who was well on his way to being discarded by the rest of society. Today, Charlie Hummert is in the Navy and reported to be doing fine.

Success with Charlie bolstered Montanari's own self-confidence. But, despite attention from the local press, the Opti-Mrs. and other civic groups, he continued to be dismissed by his critics as a nobody, a pretender, a do-it-yourselfer. Success with Charlie was not enough. Public and professional resistance crumbled slowly. In 1955, Montanari had enrolled no more than half a dozen residential and about twenty day students. He refused no child whom he thought he could help and, invariably, these were children who had been written off by the very people who criticized Montanari's methods. This was the irony.

He still had no credentials.

IV

A RANDOM SAMPLING OF THE children enrolled at the Clinical School makes dramatically clear the uncommon degree of hard work, understanding and devotion necessary to effect even minimal progress. The youngsters stand out in shocking contrast to the environment—the sun-drenched streets lined with palm trees, the gay excitement of the Hialeah racetrack with its host of pink flamingos, and the never-never land of Miami Beach just minutes away across picturesque Biscayne Bay.

Here is Timmy. He is eleven, round and fat because he eats continuously to pacify the demon of disturbance which haunts him. For breakfast he devours two full loaves of bread. He is fed as much as he desires because both Monty and the attending pediatrician agree that it is more important to avoid upsetting the delicate balance of the child's emotions than to attempt to control his appetite.

Timmy had been classified as mentally retarded but, interestingly enough, no evidence of retardation had been suggested by Timmy's kindergarten teacher or the family doctor. However, after the boy had entered grade school, his parents separated. From that time, Timmy had been shuttled back and forth between his mother and father, frequently used as a pawn by both for their own ends. Almost simultaneously with the split in the family, Timmy was found by his teachers to be "slow in learning, disinterested and withdrawn."

Still, it was not Timmy's inability to learn that drove his mother to seek help for the boy. It was the embarrassment he caused her by his habit of tearing his clothes, ripping the buttons off his shirt and carefully undoing the seams of his jackets and trousers. He engaged in this kind of compulsive behavior at home, at the movies, when visiting and while sitting in class at school. No amount of cajoling, entreaty or threat of punishment seemed to penetrate. Timmy would just look blank and resume ripping away at his clothes.

"I didn't care why he had to tear his clothes apart," Montanari comments dryly in reviewing the case. "The psychiatrists and psychologists could worry about that. All I cared about was getting him to stop. Now, I knew I couldn't make him stop just by saying, 'Timmy, cut out that kind of stuff.' So I studied him. I let him go on ripping things up. I'd watch him go behind a big eucalyptus tree in the yard and sit down there in a shady spot, then painstakingly search out the beginning of a seam and pick at the thread with his teeth. When it began to unravel, he'd smile to himself and just pull away at the thread. Every day he came back inside with his clothes in shreds. This was his way of being destructive, you see. And what I had to do was figure out how to teach him to be constructive without ignoring his special need, his preoccupation with his clothes."

One afternoon, when Timmy returned to his room with his clothes in tatters, he found Monty there, his own shirt ripped, a needle and thread in his hand. "Hi, Tim," Monty greeted the boy casually. " I hope you don't mind my sitting here on your bed. The light's better here for sewing, you see, and I tore my shirt and have to fix it. Take a look here. See, it's a pretty tricky job, threading a needle and sewing, but I kind of like it. It's a lot of fun. Only thing, you need a lot of light to do this job right. And you have more light here than anybody else in the house."

Fascinated, the boy watched Montanari, but said nothing. After a few minutes of sewing, Monty bit at the thread with his teeth to break it off and told him, "I've got to get back to work now, Tim. I'll finish this tomorrow, OK?"

Carefully, Monty took pains to stick the needle through his shirt pocket. "I didn't want to leave it around," he explains. "I

figured I'd made my point. I'd planted a thought in his mind.
That's all I wanted to do because otherwise he might get suspicious and think I was trying to put something over on him.
I was, of course. I was trying to manipulate him but I didn't
want him to suspect it. You'd be surprised how sharp these kids
can be. They'll outfox you if you don't take it slow, real slow."

Every couple of days for the next two weeks, Monty would
find excuses to drop into Timmy's room to do some sewing either
for himself or for one of the other boys at the school. But at no
time did he suggest that Timmy try to emulate him. That had to
come from the boy himself. "All I could do was try to stimulate
him," says Monty. "The motivation had to come from Timmy.
He had to *want* to try his hand with a needle and thread. So I
just bided my time and waited until he came around."

When Timmy finally "came around," he reached out for the
needle and thread which Monty was about to use for sewing
another boy's dungarees. "Betcha I can do it better 'n you,
Monty," said Timmy. He grabbed the needle from Monty's hand
without waiting for an answer and started to sew up the torn
seam of his pants.

"I didn't walk out on him then," says Monty, "because I knew
he was going to have trouble. And I didn't want him to fail,
because then he'd just give up, you see? So I stuck around and
encouraged him. 'Hey,' I said, 'you're doing better than me,
Tim. . . . Go on, just pull that needle through the cloth, that's
right. . . . See, there you go, now look how nicely that thread is
holding those old pants together.' When I finally left the boy
to himself, I told him he could hang on to that needle and
thread if he liked, that I had lots more, all kinds of thread, lots
of pretty colors, and that he could have any color he wanted.
Well, he was so busy by that time, so interested in what he was
doing, that he didn't even answer me and that's how I knew I
was getting somewhere finally."

Timmy continued to tear his clothes but now he immediately
rushed back to his room to sew the torn parts together. Soon it
became obvious that he was tearing his clothes not for a purely
destructive purpose, but constructively, as an excuse to sew the
pieces together again. As the weeks rolled by, he acquired a

collection of variously colored spools of thread and different-size needles. He took great delight in making his repairs in a variety of colors. Soon after, he lost interest altogether in ripping up his clothes and sought, instead, the torn clothes of other classmates that he might mend. He became so adept at this occupation that he became known to everyone as "Timmy the Tailor."

This proved to be the turning point in his therapy and education. He went from sewing to cutting and pasting together pictures, then to putting together jigsaw puzzles of a simple nature. As his actions became more constructive, his mental attitude brightened. He began, at last, to absorb classroom material. He was almost two years behind his own age group but began to catch up rapidly. In class, he spoke up, voiced his feelings and assumed the behavior of a "normal" child.

"All of a sudden, he wasn't retarded anymore," chuckles Montanari reflectively. "That goddamn needle and thread did it. Tim wasn't scared anymore. He had an ego. Don't ask me why it happened because I can't explain it clinically. All I know is that Tim came out of his shell and was able to be discharged. He went back home to mama and returned to public school."

Far more disturbed and complicated was Doris, an attractive fourteen-year-old whose physical development made her appear years older. Doris was seductive and charming but emotionally immature. "She is obsessed with sex," wrote one of several psychiatrists who had examined her. "While her behavior will probably never be a model of social acceptability and while the degree of emotional deprivation and trauma of her early life can never be completely counteracted, Doris does have a capacity for some positive change."

Doris' mother was blatantly promiscuous and there is reason to believe that men who solicited her mother's favors found opportunity to fondle Doris long before she reached puberty. The child's father had been married and divorced three times before he met and married Doris' mother. In retrospect, it appears that the marriage between Doris' parents was based not so much on true affection as on the false hope that marriage would provide solutions for their individual difficulties. For both parents were the products of emotionally deprived homes

and they sought to save themselves through marriage and parent-
hood. But the marriage was destined to fail and was formally
dissolved in the divorce courts soon after Doris was born. So
notorious was the mother's promiscuity that Doris was entrusted
by the court to the custody of the father. Unfortunately, he also
ignored his paternal obligations.

"This man was an absolute sonofabitch," says Montanari,
obviously agitated by his discussion of the case. "He and that
little girl lived in a trailer. He drove her around to nudist
colonies with him and let her be prematurely stimulated. He
had circuses in that trailer and that little girl was around all the
time. Now, I can't swear to this, but Doris has told me that when
she was just a little kid, her daddy used to play with her breasts
and that he seduced her. She said that he called her 'Daddy's
best girl' and that the two of them used to perform fellatio and
cunnilingus together. Now what the hell kind of a father is
that?"

Montanari admits that this is a delicate point, that children
have been known to conjure up fantastic accusations against
their parents for purely emotional reasons. But this is what
Doris reported to one of her teachers in public school.

"I had a lot of problems with my father," she is quoted as
saying. "He used to get fresh with me, make me do things back
to him, y' know. And when I wouldn't, he'd force me, make me
take off my clothes for him, and if I still wouldn't do things,
he'd beat me. There's a hole in the wall of the trailer this big
where my head went through."

When confronted with these accusations, her father denied
everything and told the authorities that Doris was just making
it all up.

"I still can't say for sure whether or not Doris was fantasizing,"
Monty says, "but I do know that a doctor examined her when
she was only ten years old and admitted that she'd been penetrated. He didn't say by whom, of course, just said it was very
slight and to forget about it, which is a hell of a thing for a
doctor to do, in my opinion. And then later on along comes a
psychiatrist who interviews Doris. Here is his report: 'In my
experience, children molested by their fathers feel deeply

ashamed of such things and only reveal them after the utmost persuasion.' Well, maybe so. Maybe Doris is a pathological liar. But we know for a fact that some of her daddy's friends whom she also accused of molesting her were picked up by the police for molesting other children. And we know that just a year before she came here to the school, Doris was molested by an old man in her neighborhood and that the principal of the school refused to press charges because he felt it would hurt what he called 'the reputation of one of the town's most reliable citizens.' That's how little he thought of Doris. He actually blamed the child for letting the old bastard make out with her!"

Eventually, Doris was taken away from her father by the juvenile authorities on the basis of what she had told her school teacher and as a result of her principal's condemnation. She was sent to a child-guidance clinic. There, the staff psychologist tried his best to help her but finally gave up. He reports: "While her sexual preoccupations are in good part a response to her natural adolescent urges, they also seem to express her feelings that the significant male figure in her life has not really loved her."

"When I finally got her," says Monty, "the only thing that mattered to me was the way she felt, the fact that she made such accusations against her father and other people, not whether or not she was telling the truth. I mean, here she was thirteen and so sick that she was being called a nymphomaniac—I personally hate labels like that—and all mixed up sexually."

Doris had no control over her primitive impulses. Whenever an adult male came into sight, she would ogle him. Then she would stick her finger in her mouth and stab repeatedly at her cheek, making a sound like "Gloop gloop gloop," while her left leg would stamp up and down in wild excitement. Suddenly, she would draw herself erect, emit an ear-piercing shriek and pounce upon the startled man. Rubbing herself hard against him and panting heavily, she would scream in ecstasy at the top of her voice.

"I tried everything to distract this child from acting-out sexually," recalls Monty, "but I got nowhere. In desperation, I consulted with a psychologist whom I knew well but who refused to work with me. He said he didn't have the time to meet with Doris, so I tried to describe her actions to him. I remember saying to him, 'What would you do if this girl came at you out of nowhere, jumped on you and began rubbing against you?' And he just laughed and said, 'Screw her!' Well, I got pretty mad. I didn't need him to tell me that. Any fool could do that. It didn't take any brains for that kind of therapy. So he became a little ashamed of himself and finally agreed to stop by and meet Doris."

The psychologist appeared unexpectedly one afternoon and sprawled out in an old easy chair while Monty went out to fetch Doris. He was so relaxed that he did not notice her entrance. Before he was quite aware of what was happening, Doris had leaped upon him, squealing with high excitement as she rubbed herself against him.

Monty had just come through the door when he heard the psychologist yelling, "Oh, my God, get this maniac off me! What do I have to do to get her off me?"

And Monty yelled back, his own voice filled with anger, "Well, goddamn it, you told me what to do, now I dare you to go on and try it yourself!"

He then rushed over, lifted Doris off the stunned psychologist and as he says in recounting the incident, "I threw him right the hell out of here!"

Because nobody wanted to help him with Doris, Montanari was forced to develop his own technique for rehabilitating this disturbed girl. "She used to threaten that by the time she reached eighteen, she'd be the biggest bum in the world," recalls Monty. "And honest to God, sometimes I found myself thinking that maybe she really would, poor soul. Maybe the child was just too far gone. And I remember thinking how I'd rather have her grow up to be a high-class call girl than an alcoholic or a dope addict or a suicide. Because she was that sick."

She passed notes to the older boys at the school offering herself sexually in order to command their attention. One such note reads: "Dear George darling: My girlfriend told me she wants to do it with you but she does not love you like I do. If you want to do it with me, I know you will like what you do to me and I will like it too because I love you. Your friend, Doris."

She masturbated frequently, and Montanari had her checked regularly by a pediatrician to be sure that she wasn't hurting herself physically. After a while, Montanari came up with the idea of having Doris sleep in a bed that squeaked. "I discovered that she didn't like for anybody to notice that she played with herself," he explains, "and I figured that maybe with a squeaky bed, she'd make noise and give herself away. It worked. And to this very day, we still use such techniques. We call it 'masking.' We place something or somebody between a child and a situation that the child has not yet learned to handle. It's an indirect way of putting a stop to an unhealthy habit."

But Doris had to have something to keep her hands busy. "You can't take something away," points out Montanari, "without replacing it with something else. I noticed that Doris liked to fuss around with her hair, so I bought her curlers and all kinds of lotions and encouraged her to do the hair of the other girls. Pretty soon, she became our number-one beautician and, little by little, transferred her interest from sex to hairdos."

It required months of patient weaning. Doris was sent to a local beauty school for more precise training and began to show so much interest that she was given an opportunity to work for a license as a practicing beautician. It was a long, hard pull and required constant encouragement. For many months she remained at the Clinical School while filling a job in downtown Miami as an apprentice beautician. She worked without salary on a commission-and-tips basis. Doris was well into her sixteenth year before Montanari considered her well enough to leave the school. By this time, she was able to support herself and move into her own little apartment with two older girls.

Doris remained highly sexed but was able to give and accept affection. Her promiscuity gave way to an urgent need to possess a male figure who shared her own intense sexual appetite. Just after her seventeenth birthday, she married a boy whom she had been dating steadily for almost a year. Before another year had passed, she gave birth to a son, whom she named Monty.

"I keep my fingers crossed for kids like Doris," says Montanari. "As far as I know, her marriage has worked out and her son is growing up with all the love that she herself never experienced in her childhood. I don't think she'll break down. She and her husband have a good relationship sexually and that's probably the most important thing for somebody like Doris. She's still working, and likes her job. I hope it keeps on that way. But with emotionally disturbed kids, you never can tell. They're living on the razor's edge. One minute they're OK and the next minute they're sicker than ever. So far, Doris is making out fine. What I think is that when she gets older, loses her youth, you know, then she may have trouble. But she has a lot of insight into herself and I think she'll come through all right."

He has learned to temper enthusiasm with caution, and backstops his basic idealism with a sharp awareness of reality. The one thing he does not strive for is perfection, for he feels that to be an impossible, unrealistic goal.

"People who think a good mental-health program must include everything before you start," he maintains, "wind up doing nothing. You have to start somewhere. You can't expect Utopia."

For kids such as "Timmy the Tailor" and Doris, he had to plead for additional funds from the Opti-Mrs., the local Lions Club, the Rotary Club, the Kiwanis and other organizations. He denied nothing to indigent children. He bought them clothes, gave them spending money and purchased medical care for them with the same devotion that he extended to his own children.

When he played in a sand pile with a little girl who was not quite in touch with life, his own daughter, Cissy—six years old at the time—joined in the play. Cissy was a delightful child, full of the devil in a healthy way. Her positive qualities rubbed off on her less fortunate playmates while she learned to accept deviant behavior as something regrettable but perfectly natural.

Montanari's son, Gary, who was then almost eight, participated even more enthusiastically in play with the younger boys. He found great joy in trying to establish relationships with some of the disturbed boys who lived in his father's house and attended the Clinical School. His friskiness, his ready grin and his natural warmth made him acceptable to these children. Gary took a particular fancy to a schizophrenic boy, three years his senior, whose given name was Rodney but who became better known as "Rod the Rememberer."

Although Rod had great difficulty relating to reality, he was blessed with an astonishing and unusual memory for dates, personal or historical. In Monty's file are transcripts of incident after incident when Rod was asked to tell the day of the week on which a particular date would fall. Gary, especially, loved to toss dates at Rod so that he could test his uncanny ability.

"What day was February 16, 1955?" asked Gary.

"Wednesday!" answered Rod in a singsong voice after a slight pause.

"Right!" said Gary. "Now see if you can tell me on what day February 16 will fall in ten years, in 1965?"

A longer pause this time, and then Rod replied triumphantly, "Tuesday!"

He was right again, as he was most of the time.

"This boy studied calendars," Montanari explains. "For some crazy reason that nobody quite understood, he retained dates in his mind. If you asked him on what day Christmas would come in a couple of years, chances are that he'd know. He got a great kick out of doing this and liked to be shown off to visitors. They thought he was some kind of genius but, believe me, Rod was a very sick boy."

When Rod drew pictures in class, they were pictures of monsters and of human internal organs, typical of the schizophrenic personality. He spent hours standing on a chair before the blackboard drawing zigzag lines, then filling in the spaces with the side of the chalk.

Frequently he walked about with a light bulb in his hand. The bulb was not connected to any wire, not plugged in, but he maintained that he needed it to help light his way. Sometimes he sat in the trunk of a gnarled old Florida holly tree in the yard, staring off into space and counting voltages while holding tightly to his light bulb. He would begin with 110 volts, then go on to 111, 112 and so on until he became exhausted. Sometimes, he would go on for as long as fourteen hours.

When Rod's parents brought him to the Montanari School, his mother told Monty, "Rod hasn't been himself for years. He began to act strangely when he was in second grade. We brought him to one doctor after another and they kept pacifying me. I was getting tired of being patted on the shoulder and being told not to worry. The doctors told my husband that it was I who needed attention and so I was the one who was given all sorts of pills to take to calm my nerves. But this didn't help Rod. The physicians—they weren't psychologists or psychiatrists—were wrong. Rod got worse and finally we had to take him out of school."

Rod had gone from being eccentric to being compulsive. He touched things, walked on tiptoe, repeated words over and over to himself. By the time his parents took him to see a clinical psychologist, his personality was beginning to disintegrate seriously.

"He came to me first as a day student," says Montanari, "because the family lived close by. The psychologist who'd examined him said he suffered from 'childhood schizophrenia' and he blamed it on some weakness in the boy, because the home environment seemed good. The parents seemed interested in the child's welfare. But I've never been quite convinced of this. Rod's parents were nice people but, somehow, I got the feeling that they were holding something back, that things were not quite as normal as they suggested. It was just a feeling and I never did find out if I was right or wrong. I concentrated on doing something for the boy."

Rod was remarkable. He never did anything destructive. He had very good manners. Unlike other children who came storming into Monty's office demanding to see him, Rod knocked first at the door, then announced politely, "I am looking for an appointment to speak to that dedicated man!" And Monty admits, with a shy grin, that it did wonders for his own ego.

As a day student, the boy was getting nowhere. He was, in fact, getting worse. He had begun to retreat more and more from reality and had developed the habit of walking through the yard on tiptoe, in his bare feet, chasing imaginary butterflies. At this point, Montanari convinced the boy's parents that Rod should remain at the school as a residential student, for he felt it was important that he be removed temporarily from his home environment. The parents agreed.

Montanari decided to try to remake Rod's delusion of chasing nonexistent butterflies into something positive by persuading him to chase real butterflies. He encouraged him to collect specimens and to show them off to the other children. This seemed to have a salutary effect on the boy's self-image, and to help snap him back to reality. At that point, Montanari decided that Rod could profit from supplementary psychotherapy. His parents could afford the extra cost and so he arranged to have the boy visit a psychoanalyst three times a week.

"I worked with him my way and the psychoanalyst worked with him his way," says Monty. "We helped one another. I knew we were getting somewhere when, one day, Rod stood on a square of the sidewalk in front of the school and said to me, 'Y' know, Monty, I'm the only person in the whole world who is on this square.' Frankly, I had never thought about it before but suddenly I got the feeling that Rod was establishing his own feeling of self-importance in this world. He was beginning to feel that he counted and was comparing himself to other kids. He was getting in touch with reality."

When Rod was finally returned home, he was what Montanari calls an "ambulatory schiz." He was still schizophrenic but able to function, to get along in society. He was able to absorb some learning, to do things for himself, to relate to other children. He continued in psychoanalysis but the sessions were reduced to once a week. He returned to public school, where he was enrolled in a special class, then moved into a regular class the following term.

"The tragic thing about this boy, and others like him, was that he was basically a very brilliant youngster," says Montanari sadly. "He just was unable to make the most of his abilities. Personally, I thank God that he improved as much as he did. For a long time, he wrote long letters to me and dropped by to say hello when he was in the neighborhood with his parents. But, you know, a funny thing happened to Rod. The more he became adjusted to reality, the less able he was to remember dates the way he used to. It's my guess that he found less need to do this kind of thing once he began to feel sure of his own identity. He isn't 'Rod the Rememberer' anymore; he's just Rod the human being, and I often tell my staff about him. It seems to pick them up to hear about a boy like this and, you know, when you're dealing with disturbed kids, it's damned important to work with a staff that's inspired, not just capable."

It has been acknowledged by professional people who know him that Montanari has a remarkable talent for selecting an effective staff. This is a field where good staff members—teachers or house parents—are hard to find. Generally, the best are expensive, scarce and subject to a high rate of turnover. Those with academic qualifications in psychology or social work are scarcer still. So Montanari has had to substitute ingenuity and intuitive judgment in gathering a staff together, seeking qualifications other than academic training from the people he employs.

Recently, at a symposium on troubled children at Florida Atlantic University, when asked, "Where do you find the people who work with you?" Monty replied in characteristic manner, "Under every bush and every rock. I look, especially, for people who have had some parallel experiences. One of our most successful house mothers, for instance, is a former lab technician. She's had a lot of book learning in her field and knows how to tackle medical problems. So I gave her a cottage that has a lot of medication. There's a diabetic boy, a boy who's epileptic, a boy with a lot of allergies; and she gets involved in the medical part under the supervision of the pediatrician, the psychiatrist and the head nurse. But she has other qualities, too. You see, most of my staff aren't academic people, yet they do superb jobs. An academic degree has a lot to add to a person's qualifications, but not in isolation. I mean, you don't prepare yourself for this field in four years at college just studying in a class about disturbed children. You have to touch them, to feel them. In biology, for example, you don't just read about a frog; you handle the frog with your bare hands and then you come out knowing the frog much better than if you just looked it up in a book. It's even more important, working with troubled kids, to actually live with such children and become involved in their problems. How else are you going to know what irritates you? Not from a book! Because you react differently when you come into actual contact with such a child. Let's say he hits you. Well, how do you react? And then, how do you react tomorrow? And the day after tomorrow? These kids keep testing you, trying your patience. Once they learn how to manipulate you and get away with it, they win the battle but lose the war. So you can't let this happen. It isn't good for the child and that's all that counts, as far as I'm concerned. I don't care what's good for you, I care about what's good for the child. And this is something you don't get out of books, no matter how many degrees you have trailing after your name."

Mrs. Chellie Estes is the mother of six children. Born in Waynesboro, Mississippi, she struggled hard for an education and managed to reach Alcorn A. & M. College where she majored in education. But she could not complete her college education. She married young, raised a family, worked while attending college, but then her husband became ill. Part-time work was not enough. In Mississippi, she could not find an adequate full-time job, so the family piled into their old second-hand car and came to Florida, in search of better opportunities. At the church that they attended, Chellie heard of a job opening at the Montanari School. She applied and was accepted. The job was that of a maid. Today Chellie Estes is the principal of the intermediate division of the school. But more important is the fact that Chellie Estes is a Negro.

Here, in Hialeah, in the heart of the South, she supervises white children and their white adult teachers. She is able to do this for two reasons. The first one is that she is highly qualified for the task, warmly understanding of children and of a gentle but firm disposition that commands respect from the white adults under her supervision. The second is that Montanari continually buoys up her self-confidence with frequent demonstrations of his own respect for her abilities and an adamant refusal to countenance objections from parents, neighbors or staff members on purely racial grounds.

"Mr. Monty"—as she calls him—"made it possible for me to give my own children the education that I never did succeed in getting for myself," she says. "I will never forget how he came over to me one afternoon when I was cleaning up some child's room and said to me, 'Chellie, one of these days I'm going to give you a teaching job.' I laughed, because I just couldn't believe he could mean what he said. I knew what trouble he was going through himself and I knew that this was still the South and to most people I was black and that's all. But one day, Mr. Monty came over to me and said, 'Chellie, I want you to take over this class and teach them, will you do that?' Well, I was pretty surprised and very grateful. I took over that class, teaching them while I was still working as a maid at the school and still had on my maid's uniform. Then, after a few weeks, Mr. Monty came over to me and said, 'Chellie, you are too good a teacher to waste your time and the children's time as a maid. Go on, take off your uniform. From now on, you're just going to teach.' I remember feeling very happy then but worried that it would hurt Mr. Monty because I think I was the only Negro teacher in all of Florida at that time. But he said to me, 'Chellie, this is my school and I'll do what I want. You go on and teach.' He stood up for me all the time."

There were children who said to her, "You're a nigger, and you can't tell me what to do!" There were parents who balked at permitting her to touch their offspring, complaining to Monty, "Don't you let her put her black hands on my kid!"

But Montanari refused to be intimidated. Chellie was an excellent teacher and good for the children. He told her to disregard these remarks and, by his faith, encouraged her to accept racial insults in the same way that a white teacher was obliged to accept nonracial insults. Chellie says that very few children made reference to her color but, when they did, she learned to ignore being called "a fuckin' black bitch" by a disturbed child just as Ruth or Jim Griffin, or even Monty himself, had become immune to similar nasty remarks without the racial overtones.

Soon after Chellie was advanced from maid to teacher, her mettle was tested by Gloria, an intensely disturbed twelve-year-old girl who was referred to by her mother as "it." In a letter to Montanari prior to Gloria's enrollment, the mother wrote: "If anyone is going to change, it has to be *it*. *It* is impossible to put up with. *It* upsets me so much I try to hide when *it* comes into the room. I simply cannot love *it*. This screwy kid is ruining my marriage. *It*'s sister is fine, *it*'s brother is fine but *it* is more than I can stand. You are our last hope. Can you help *it*?"

Gloria was a tall, skinny girl with frizzled brown hair. She was terribly angry at her parents, herself and society in general. Twice in her young lifetime, she had attempted to stab herself to death with a pair of kitchen shears.

"Gloria wasn't brain-damaged, wasn't schizophrenic, wasn't anything except terribly disturbed," Montanari says. "She wasn't pretty, had a miserable personality and couldn't get along with anybody. She just had nothing going for her."

The girl had been seen by a psychologist and psychiatrist in the area for testing and treatment. Both felt that Gloria required intensive therapy in a tight-security residential treatment center and, even then, were pessimistic as to her prognosis. Of particular interest to Montanari was the fact that he had been trying, without success, to attract both of these professionals to his side as consultants, but they would have nothing to do with him.

"In a way, I was lucky when Gloria's mama brought her child here," says Monty. "I had an opportunity to prove what I could do with a very sick child and impress these doctors, you see. Besides, I didn't think Gloria was as impossible as everybody made her out to be. And, quite honestly, I couldn't afford to fail with Gloria because her folks were paying me my full fee of three hundred dollars a month and, my God, how I needed the money."

Chellie became Gloria's teacher and Montanari was hopeful that this woman's remarkable patience would allow her to cope with the child's anger and hate. But before Gloria had completed her first day at the school, she had deluged Chellie with a stream of filthy language and had even attempted to poison her.

The poisoning attempt was clever. So clever, in fact, that if it were not for the intensity of Chellie's interest in the children placed in her class, Gloria may well have succeeded. For, without being observed, she had broken into the medicine chest in the upstairs bathroom and had stolen a bottle of phenobarbital.

Again, without being observed, she had dumped the bottle of pills into a glass of water, and casually offered Chellie the glass during lunchtime.

"I don't know exactly why, but I became suspicious," recalls Chellie. "I guess Gloria seemed too eager when she shoved that glass at me. I remember looking at it pretty carefully and noticing that the water was cloudy. It didn't occur to me that the child was actually trying to poison me. I thought she'd just put something in it to make it taste bad, that's all. So I said, 'No, thanks, Gloria, I'm not really thirsty.' Then suddenly she got real mad and began to scream at me."

"Damn you, damn you," she screamed, "I wanted you to drink this stuff so that you could go to sleep. Then, while you were asleep, I could shove some dirt up your vagina to give you an infection!"

This is the sort of girl that Gloria was. She acted out her aggressions. When she was angry, she let everybody know it. One day, she walked into Monty's office, her face grim, and yanked the typewriter from his desk, slamming it to the floor. Another time, she grabbed a rock and tossed it through the windshield of Monty's car.

She carried a scissors with her at all times. In class, she drew pictures of a male and female who seemed to represent her parents and then stuck her scissors into the pictures and cut off the parts that represented heads, arms and legs. In laborious printing, she labeled the pictures "dirty mice."

It was Chellie who absorbed most of her aggression. But the teacher allowed her to act out her deepest feelings. "Whatever she did or said, I knew she didn't intend it personally for me," explains Chellie. "Gloria was just all full of hate and she had to let go at somebody. If it wasn't me, it would have been somebody else. She kept on cussin' me and I kept on smiling until one day she said to me, 'Chellie, nothing ever seems to bother you!' When I told Mr. Monty about this, he laughed and said, 'Chellie, I think at last you're beginning to reach her.' And that's just what was happening. Pretty soon, I began to see that the more she cussed at me, the more she began to trust me, same as she did Mr. Monty, because neither of us made any demands of her. We just didn't expect her to be any different from the way that she was. If she was going to change, it would have to be because she wanted to, that's all."

Dr. Eugene Bird, who serves on the staff of the Dade County Child Guidance Clinic, is the psychologist who had examined Gloria and recommended residential treatment, but not with Montanari. "I had been taught that only a professional person could teach an emotionally disturbed child," he says candidly, "so I refused to have anything to do with Monty at that time. I wouldn't answer his phone calls, wouldn't see him and certainly wouldn't send a patient to him."

Dr. Steven Wright, a well-known child psychiatrist in private practice in the area, was the psychiatrist who had seen Gloria. For two years, Montanari had endeavored to enlist his services on behalf of his children. "I all but laughed in his face," confesses Dr. Wright with a chuckle. "He was terribly persistent and I remember telling my nurse to slam the door in his face when he came around to see me. For, at that time, I agreed with my colleagues that it made no sense to tie up with a man who had no professional credentials."

After several months, when Gloria began to show improvement of a noticeable nature, Montanari again contacted Dr. Bird and Dr. Wright. But now he piqued their interest, for he was talking about a child with whom they were familiar. "If you want to see what I've done with Gloria," he told them, "come on over and take a look."

One afternoon, Dr. Bird stopped by. "I was amazed," he recalls, "at the change. She was a different girl emotionally, socially, even physically. She even looked better. I was so impressed that I agreed to work with Monty and do psychological evaluations for his kids."

Dr. Wright was more difficult to convince but he, too, finally opened his door to Monty. "I took one look at Gloria," he recalls, "and could hardly believe my eyes. When I had first seen this girl, she was almost inaccessible. It was impossible to communicate with her. Now, suddenly, here she stood in front of me, a lively human being. I spent a good deal of time with Monty then, talking things over, and discovered that he was working with the guts of the thing over there. I mean, to his kind of kids, I was just another member of the foster-home gang or the court or the welfare department, just some sort of fink. But to them Monty was a real person, not a doctor, and they needed to learn how to live more than they needed the kind of help I could give them. So I went over to the school and examined his set-up. He had the non-doers, the discipline problems, the pre-delinquents, the runaways, the acter-outers. These were kids who had difficulty relating to parents or parent surrogates—psychiatrists, for example, and probation officers and truant officers—because they felt they never really had a fair shake as far as their upbringing was concerned. Well, I found it hard to believe what I saw, how this man, a plain ordinary teacher, was making things happen with kids like Gloria."

Now, with Dr. Bird and Dr. Wright in his corner, Montanari's professional life began to take a turn for the better. Ironically, however, his private life was taking a turn for the worse. His relationship with his wife had been deteriorating for some time, increasing in direct proportion to the amount of time and attention that Monty poured into his work. After twelve years of marriage, it became clear that the two had reached the point of no return.

"Our goals were too far apart," comments Ann Montanari, an attractive woman with a charming Southern accent. She considers her former husband "smart, brilliant in psychology and very wise," but adds, "I honestly don't think he can handle normal children."

This was part of their conflict. Religion was another. "Going to church means a lot to me," says Ann Montanari, "but putting my husband into organized religion was like trying to put an illiterate into college."

For Monty was not raised to be a churchgoer. His father says, "Last confession I made on my own willin' was in 1912. I got religion: don' ever do to others what you don' want 'em to do to you. Ain't that religion?"

Monty's formal religious training was as elementary as that. "I couldn't find in church the same kind of peace of mind that Ann could find," says Monty. "I found it in my work, in helping

kids who couldn't help themselves. This was, and still is, my religion, trying to help the less fortunate. But if I didn't trust in
God, I don't think I could help anybody at all."

He became terribly upset by the disruption of his marriage
and the need to establish formal visits with his two children.
But his own emotional life had to be thrust into the background
because his work began to make even greater demands upon
him. Even as his divorce came through, he was involved with
the problem of dealing with a pair of teen-agers whose adolescence had gone haywire. Their personal difficulties made them
the strangest of sweethearts and, in their peculiar relationship,
they found the answer to their very private problems.

V

VISITORS TO THE CLINICAL SCHOOL were immediately charmed by Evelyn Loeb, a sultry-eyed, rosy-cheeked fifteen-year-old with an ingratiating smile. Well-groomed, soft-spoken and genteel in manner, she appeared to be the very essence of femininity.

"People used to come over to me and say, 'What is that girl doing here? There's nothing the matter with her, she's as normal as I am,'" Montanari recalls. "But this wasn't really Evelyn. This was the way Evelyn *wanted* to be. She was a beautiful child and doctors told me that her fine physical features were her only bridge to people. You see, Evelyn doted on her appearance but didn't believe that she was pretty at all. She kept looking at herself in the mirror, trying to convince herself that she was worthwhile as a female. She did this so often that she became known to my staff and me as 'the girl in the mirror.'"

A full-length mirror was attached to the inner door of the closet in Evelyn's room. When her roommates were out, it was her habit to sit, nude, on a stool before the mirror, a hairbrush in one hand and eyebrow tweezers in the other, and gaze for hours at her reflection. Now and then she would interrupt her fixed stare—an "almost catatonic state," a psychiatrist called it —to brush her hair or pluck at her eyebrows. To her roommates, she was "stuck up"; to doctors who interrogated her, she was "narcissistic and homosexual"; and to herself, she was simply "awful lonely."

Her behavior puzzled Montanari, for she was quite different from other children with whom he had worked. She had been referred to him by the Children's Service Bureau of Dade County, and he accepted her for residential treatment because the Bureau had exhausted all other possibilities of assistance, and because he found a purely personal, emotional challenge in Evelyn.

Dr. Steven Wright, the child psychiatrist with whom Montanari had finally effected a professional relationship, explains Monty's acceptance or rejection of a child, then as now, in this way:

The child must appeal to him in order for him to accept that child for reeducation and therapy. The child must offer a substantial challenge to him. For it is almost as if every child is entering into individual personal therapy with Mr. Montanari rather than simply entering the clinical school. He doesn't share the tendency of many workers in the field to gravitate toward the so-called easy cases. He looks deeper for the potential in the child and for the personal challenge presented by that child's problem. What it boils down to is that he himself has to be motivated emotionally in order to take on the child.

It would not be incorrect to say that in being true to himself, Monty becomes true to the child. From the emotional need that compels him to accept the child, he derives the strength and insight that enable him to form a workable relationship with such a youngster and to welcome the challenge of obstacles that overwhelm most of his colleagues.

When Monty found himself unable to plumb the depths of Evelyn's attachment to the mirror, he took her on long walks, bought her ice-cream sodas at the neighborhood drugstore and when she stood by herself in the schoolyard, he engaged her in long conversations.

"It was no trouble getting her to talk," says Montanari, "and when these children talk, it's important to listen even if they're only fantasizing. Evelyn loved to pour herself out to me and she could use the filthiest language in such a nice, sweet way that you began to wonder if you heard her right."

Here is a transcript of a typical conversation. Montanari asks, "Did you look into the mirror today, Evelyn?"

"I look in the mirror every day," she replies. "When I'm upset, I spend more time in the mirror."

"Why, Evelyn? Does it make you feel better?"

"In a way, I guess it does," she answers. "But sometimes I wish I could smash the shitty mirror because I hate it sometimes, and then I love it sometimes. Because when I go into the mirror, I think to myself, people don't want me in the mirror, but I keep going back and forth into it trying to persuade myself I'm a real girl. I want to leave the shitty mirror lots of times, Monty, but I can't."

"Why not? What do you see there?"

"I don't know. I'm not really thinking about my face so much or my body, I don't think. I'm all naked but I just keep looking, not really seeing myself. I'm thinking about other things, other girls, other people, all men and even women, I guess. Mainly, I think, I just want to stand there and keep trying to look at myself and persuade myself that I'm nice for somebody else to look at."

At this point, Evelyn begins to cry and Monty asks her gently if she would rather drop the conversation. "No," she answers quickly, "I have to talk about my problems even though they upset me, because I want to be helped."

Such remarks convinced Montanari that Evelyn had a great deal of insight into herself, and stimulated him to get to the heart of her problem so that he might help her. In a transcript of another of their conversations, he asks her, "What do you think of your looks, Evelyn? Do you think you're pretty?"

"I'm not sure," she replies uneasily. "I get upset with people who like me only for my looks because I don't think they really like me for what I really am, for me."

"What else would you like them to like you for?"

"Just for being me, an ordinary teen-ager, that's all. You know what I mean, Monty, just for being a person, a friend. But sometimes I hear my mother's voice, or my father's, here inside me, I mean, and they're telling me, 'Evelyn, you're sick because you like girls too much and that's all wrong.' And it makes me scared when I hear their voices like that."

"What do you think they mean by that, Evelyn, that you like girls too much?"

"Oh, you know. When I face a girl, it's like facing a boy. I get all excited, I want to screw with the girl, you know, and then I get scared. I feel good in a way and bad in a way. I want to be like other girls, get married and raise a family, but I'm afraid. I'd rather be liked by a boy than a girl. I'd rather screw with a boy. But I can't, I don't know why but I just can't, something holds me back."

"And with a girl, what do you feel, hm, what do you feel?"

"Sometimes I want one of the girls I know to kiss me. I want to touch her, to have her sleep under me, but then I feel terrible thinking such dirty awful things. I get guilty and it makes me sick. That's why I can't stand my mother touching me, because I feel wrong toward her, like to another girl. I remember once I felt kinda crazy and called her up and said, 'Mom, I'm coming home soon to visit you so make room in your bed for me because I feel like a boy.' And my mom got very angry with me and bawled me out for talking to her that way."

Montanari did not press her too hard. "I didn't want to dig too deep," he explains. "The psychiatrists could do that if they thought it would help her. But I found out from Chellie and Ruth Griffin other things about Evelyn that she didn't mention to me—how she'd allowed another girl to fondle her, how she sometimes took other girls' underthings to bed with her and how she seemed to feel more comfortable with tomboys. It became pretty clear that Evelyn was trying awfully hard to avoid being an overt homosexual but was having a lot of trouble resisting her impulses. What made it worse was that she was going through adolescence, a time when youngsters have to establish their sexual identity, and Evelyn had far more problems to contend with than the average adolescent. She was at a point in her development where she could go this way or that."

During this period in his career, Montanari engaged Mrs. Alver Louys, a dynamic young woman with a degree in education from Connecticut State Teachers College. Although she began as a teacher, today Alver is Monty's right-hand girl Friday in charge of all administrative detail. "Nobody ever interviewed me for a job the way Monty did," she recalls with a chuckle. "He just glanced at my college record, tossed it aside and said something like, 'I'm not really interested in how much you learned out of books, Mrs. Louys. What I want to know is what would you do if some kid came up to you and said he wants to kill you, or take you to bed, or if it was a girl who wanted to take you to bed, how would you handle a child like that?' He told me he needed somebody who wouldn't feel threatened by such far-out behavior and who'd look upon a disturbed child as being no different from one who was crippled physically. Well, I told him I'd quit teaching public school in Connecticut because I got fed up with the red tape, that I'd seen too many kids who seemed sick to me and who needed special help, but that there wasn't any such help around for them. I guess he became convinced that such kids didn't scare me, because he gave me the job."

Soon afterward, Montanari hired Mrs. Frances Hoague, who became the supervisor of house parents and became known to the youngsters at the school as Miss Frances. She was a widow who had worked with disturbed youngsters at a special school in Illinois, but had no college credentials. "I moved to Miami after my husband died," says Miss Frances, "and went to an employment agency for a job. They told me there was an opening at the Montanari Clinical School for a house mother, that the owner was a kook and not interested in college training, so maybe I could get the job. Well, I went over, was interviewed by Monty and got the job. I became Evelyn's house mother. But before my first day was over, I was complaining to Ruth Griffin about the filthy language used by this girl who had seemed to be so sweet and innocent. I didn't dare tell Monty for fear of being fired, but I found out later that word had got around to him. And he picked the most shocking way imaginable to get me used to that kind of language."

In a manner typical of Montanari, he went about "reconditioning" Miss Frances to the vulgar language used by the children. He had her work in his office one afternoon and used four-letter words over and over again. "Get this fucking desk cleaned up," he would say. "File these fucking papers, get that fucking grass in the yard cut!" With repetition, the shock began to wear off and the vulgarisms began to lose their significance. At the end of the day, he said to her, "Frances, I'm sorry if I've shocked you but this is the kind of school we have here. My kids use pretty raw language sometimes. They can't help themselves. And if you want to work with us, you just have to get used to it. It's no different from my saying, 'If you can't stand blood, how can you be a surgeon?' "

His approach succeeded and Miss Frances remained as Evelyn's house mother. Alver Louys became Evelyn's teacher and recalls, "She always seemed pleasant enough but would not do any work in class. When I asked her why, she said to me, 'Because if I don't do anything in class, you won't know if I know anything or not.' That's how little confidence she had in herself. But I always had the feeling that she was a lot smarter than she let on."

Evelyn was given a complete psychiatric work-up and the clinical evaluation underscored "three outstanding impressions from all tests administered." These impressions were: (a) "impaired emotional and intellectual development," (b) "crippling anxiety and sexual preoccupation," and (c) "overall test responses more pathological than might be expected from a girl who verbalizes so well."

Montanari says of these findings, "Don't misunderstand me, I have a great deal of respect for the doctors who spent so much time with Evelyn and administered these tests, but what does it all mean? These are things we knew all the time. If she wasn't sick emotionally, she wouldn't be here in the first place. My staff and I could tell that she had trouble with sexual identification without bothering to test her. As for her being different from other girls and her problems more pathological, well, sure, you could tell this from just talking to her. So all this expensive professional testing didn't really tell us any more than we already knew. They didn't tell us how to *help* Evelyn, which is all that I was interested in. In fact, they told me she had only a seventy-one IQ, and I frankly refused to believe it. I don't give a goddamn how she scored on her tests. I knew she was doing lousy scholastically and that she was no intellectual giant, but I just couldn't believe that a girl so alive, so aware, so sharp at times, could be subnormal. If she seemed stupid about current events, it wasn't because she was too stupid to understand but because she just didn't give a damn about what was going on. All you had to do was talk to her to see that she was only concerned about herself, not about the rest of the world. And knowing her background, it was no wonder she was all tied up in knots the way she was."

Mr. and Mrs. Loeb had been married little more than a year before Evelyn was born. She was their only offspring. Mrs. Loeb was a weak, childish woman, fifteen years younger than her husband, and terribly frightened by the demands of maternity. She compensated for her feelings of inadequacy by having boyfriends. Mr. Loeb resented the child for other reasons. He was something of a Don Juan and, by the time of Evelyn's birth, had exhausted all reasons for remaining married to his wife. A few months after Evelyn's arrival, he obtained a divorce. Because Mrs. Loeb enjoyed such a poor reputation, the child was entrusted to the father and the woman he married almost immediately after his divorce was made final.

Evelyn's stepmother resented the child. She saw her as a rival and treated her accordingly. Evelyn related several instances in which her stepmother told her she hated her because she was making affectionate gestures toward her father. On the other hand, Evelyn also related how her father, after he had separated from his second wife, threw wild parties attended by "queers" —men dressed as women—and how these people had intrigued and fascinated her. Now and then, a woman or a man—sometimes it was difficult for her to distinguish between the sexes— would fondle and stimulate her. The only normal affection she received was from her father's parents, to whose care she was occasionally entrusted.

Not until Evelyn had reached her teens did her real mother begin to express an interest in her. She, too, had remarried but this marriage had likewise proved unsuccessful. Evelyn became so concerned with her mother's finding a proper mate that she once wrote to Monty, "I sure hope that one of these days my mom finds somebody to love. I think that there is a way she can tell if she likes a man enough to marry him. She just has to light up inside. Then she'll know if it is really love."

This, in brief, was Evelyn's background. Hers was not simply a broken home; it was an intensely disturbed home. By the time she came to the attention of the authorities, the emotional damage had gone deep and was threatening to distort her character to the point where it was questionable whether she could be helped back to normalcy.

"Oh, God, did they have names for Evelyn's trouble!" remarks Montanari, shaking his head in disbelief. "Doctor after doctor examined her. Here, I'll read you their comments. They said she was suffering from 'diffuse emotional reactivity,' and 'pathological preoccupation with female genitalia,' and 'defeminization leading to incipient homosexuality.' Lots of fancy words but, as far as I'm concerned, this was all bullshit. Fancy words to describe what was wrong with Evelyn in clinical terms, but nobody bothering to explain just what the hell to do about it, what it all meant. When she was turned over to me, all I got were the fancy words and no help. I got the feeling that everybody was more interested in putting some label on this girl than trying to figure out how to help her become a decent, self-sufficient human being, and it made me goddamned sick."

His divorce and separation from his children, whom he could visit only at specific times, added to Montanari's burden. He sought release in painting. He painted pictures of the school, his home in Winchendon, Massachusetts, and, in abstractions, was able to relieve some of his pent-up emotions by the mere act of putting paint on a canvas.

He found additional release in telephone calls to his mother and father. For he remained close to his parents—especially his mother—but he never wrote; he telephoned. "Since he left home," his father remarks, "he never wrote more than five letters. Always, he telephones. He just got to hear the voice, got to have somebody to talk to."

He called home more frequently as he found himself less and less able to cope with Evelyn. Despite all his efforts, she seemed to be slipping away more and more toward homosexuality. Montanari took such disappointments personally and required constant reassurance about his own ability. Then, in what now seems a master stroke of fate, young Eugene Otis was enrolled at the school. He, too, was a teen-ager, a year older than Evelyn, and suffering from a similar problem. Now the idea occurred to Montanari that he might kill two birds with one stone, as it were, by bringing Evelyn and Eugene together.

Severely disturbed children generally appear to be younger than their years and Eugene Otis was no exception. He did not look sixteen. His build was slight, his complexion pale and his emotions flat. When he was not utterly quiet and withdrawn, he skipped about like a small child, his eyes bright and his smile refreshingly innocent. Eugene coveted cleanliness but abhorred pretentiousness. He felt most comfortable in washed-out, faded dungarees and a soft, often-laundered cotton T-shirt.

His long, sensitive fingers were forever touching, twitching, twisting themselves around one another in a nervous clasping and unclasping of the hands. And often they were busy toying with the fly of his pants or stroking his genitals or fingering the intimate belongings of other boys: a toothbrush, a pair of dirty socks, a sweat-stained jockstrap. For, like Evelyn, Eugene, too, sought refuge from his fears in sexual preoccupations that had distinct homosexual overtones.

"This boy's family moved here from Georgia," Montanari remarks, "when a psychologist recommended residential placement for Eugene. You see, they were ashamed to send him someplace closer to home. They didn't mind having him see a psychologist privately because that was a little more fashionable, and more acceptable, than putting the boy 'away,' as they expressed it. I guess you can't blame parents for feeling that way but I just wish they'd realize it's no disgrace for a child to be disturbed and that there is no shame in sending him to a residential treatment center. Instead of feeling proud that they could help their son, Mr. and Mrs. Otis felt embarrassed. So they moved here where nobody knew them."

At the time of Eugene's enrollment, Mrs. Otis told Monty only that the boy had found increasing difficulty in school and that, although not mentally retarded, he had withdrawn from participation in class to the point where he would speak only three words: "Yes," "No" and "Possibly." As a result, he had been sent to a private psychologist for therapy but, after six months of regular treatment, the psychologist had recommended residential placement for Eugene.

A lengthy report from the psychologist indicated many more problems than Mrs. Otis had suggested. "His parents showed little awareness of Eugene's developing illness," states the report. "The boy's gentle manner is misleading. He acts out his hostilities in peculiar ways. When first seen by me, he blinked almost continually, a defensive gesture to shut out the fearful visual images that ran through his mind. While being tested, he took a mother doll and beat it repeatedly. He revealed that he has often barricaded himself in his room to masturbate, urinated on the carpet, the dirty laundry and his bed. These aggressive acts and defensive maneuvers have prevented real personality disintegration in this troubled child. When he dirtied the carpet, he knew what he was doing. It was purposive, not disorganized, behavior."

The psychologist went on to explain that Mr. and Mrs. Otis' relationship was poor, devoid of both love and sex. Mrs. Otis lived in dread of aging and dressed herself in far more youthful clothes than were becoming to her. More importantly, she used Eugene, an only child, as a substitute for her husband. She took the boy along on shopping trips, solicited his opinions on her wardrobe, and generally treated him as her "little husband." Although the boy had reached the age of puberty, she continued to bathe him, to invade his privacy and to invite him to share her bed when she was in her nightclothes. "This created in Eugene a tremendous sexual conflict," the psychologist noted, "that showed up plainly in the Rorschach and other tests. It was, in essence, a conflict between his own need for love and competition with his father, who has always been a disappointment to his wife."

Monty discovered that there was more to Eugene's sexual confusion than even the psychologist had suggested. "I learned that a social worker had visited the Otis home a few times when

Eugene was still in grade school," says Montanari, "because the neighbors had complained of hearing violent fights in the home. This social worker reported that when she arrived at the home, the door was open, and that she just walked in. She said that she saw the old man on the couch with Eugene, nibbling on the child's buttocks and kissing him suggestively. She got the feeling that the old man was a repressed homosexual and this was probably what was wrong with his marriage."

If so, this seemed to be the extent of Eugene's father's interest in his son. It also became apparent soon after the boy's enrollment at the Clinical School that his mother was the dominant member of the family. These impressions were revealed by Eugene in a note he wrote to Monty. It is a neat, carefully written letter on lined paper, with many curlicues in the penmanship and careful circles over the *i*'s.

The note reads:

DEAR MONTY,

I sure am grateful for your taking me to the beach. It was a lot of fun. My dad never took me to the beach or anywheres. You know, in most families, the father is the mean one. But this isn't true in my family because my dad hardly ever punished me. It was my mother. I love her, of course, but she was mean lots of times. Sometimes I think that's why she and my dad had so many fights. The trouble with him is that he never took me anywhere like you did today. It sure felt good, being your pal. Thanks a lot. Just please don't show anybody this letter because they wouldn't understand and maybe my mom would see it and get awful mad. OK?

Eugene's hostility toward the opposite sex soon became apparent. One morning, Miss Frances went to her closet for her clothes and discovered they had been slashed to ribbons with a penknife. The evidence pointed to Eugene. When confronted by Montanari, the boy readily admitted that he had done the damage and, when asked why he had done it, replied, "I don't know. I guess because she reminded me of my mother."

On another day he was found exposing himself to several other boys, boasting about the size of his sexual organs and the amount of pubic hair surrounding them, but making no attempt to engage in overt homosexual activity. On the contrary, he was pinned against a tree one afternoon by a neighborhood boy, who was fondling Eugene's penis and was intent on initiating him into homosexuality, when they were discovered by Montanari.

Highly distraught, Eugene revealed, "He wanted me to give him a blow job and said if I didn't, he'd beat me up. Please don't let him beat me up!"

Despite Eugene's tendency toward homosexuality, he was apparently reluctant to act out his feelings. Such tendencies are not uncommon among emotionally disturbed children, nor even among "normal" children. But in the latter, they quite naturally give way to heterosexual desires. In the case of disturbed children, however, the sexual conflict frequently remains unresolved.

Even today, no one can clearly explain the basis of homosexuality or outline a clear-cut scientific method of treatment. Dr. Samuel B. Hadden, a psychiatrist who has specialized in this problem for more than a decade, recently told a conference of the American Group Psychotherapy Association that he had obtained "gratifying results" through group psychotherapy confined to male homosexuals and found, in almost every case, some kind of disturbance in the boy's relationship with his mother.

But Montanari contends, "We're still waiting for the answers to why one child is homosexual and another isn't. I've seen kids with perfectly adequate parents who turned homosexual because of competition with a sibling of the opposite sex. And I've seen kids who were raised in the kind of environment that should have turned them into homosexuals, but it didn't work that way. So maybe it isn't only environment that does it. Maybe it's something in their genes, their sensitivity, that makes them vulnerable. There just isn't one key that fits all doors and there isn't just one way of treating all kids who seem to have homosexual inclinations. Every child has to be handled differently."

It is standard practice at the Montanari School to put no fewer than three girls, or three boys, in a dormitory. The third child acts as a deterrent to the other two and prevents them from forming an unhealthy relationship. In addition, it is standard practice for the house parent to situate his bed so that a child cannot wander during the night to another's bed without the house parent's awareness.

"I admit," says Montanari, "that this is an artificial way to keep such kids out of trouble, but what else can you do? It takes time to build up the self-image of these kids. Sometimes you're able to find one child who can help another, then you're lucky. I guess I was lucky with Evelyn and Eugene. Here was a perfect example of how two negatives can make a positive."

A relationship between Evelyn and Eugene suggested itself to Montanari quite accidentally one afternoon when he was playing with the children in the yard and happened to notice an exchange of sly smiles between the two. "I had a feeling," he says, "that they had found something in common. I kept watching them. They never went near each other until the time came for them to return to their rooms to get ready for dinner. Then I noticed that Eugene would sidle over to Evelyn and very gently take her arm, leading her back into the house. That's when the idea struck me that maybe these two could do more for each other than I could do for either of them."

He became excited at the prospect and discussed his feelings with a psychologist who had interviewed Eugene. "He is a very peculiar boy," the psychologist admitted. "It might very well be a good idea to find him a girlfriend, someone timid like himself with whom he could relate and who would not threaten him. Perhaps Evelyn is such a girl."

Monty then discussed the matter with a psychiatrist who had talked to Evelyn. The doctor agreed that such a relationship might work if the sensitivity of the two youngsters overlapped in just the right way, with just enough tenderness, just enough mutual dislike of their respective backgrounds and just enough healthy sexuality to allow them to spin away from their sexual maladjustments and to find an outlet for their feelings in each other. The psychiatrist, however, was skeptical of such a possibility.

Monty, on the other hand, was optimistic. "There was nothing to lose," he explains, "by encouraging such a relationship, and these kids had everything to gain if it worked. All I had to do was see to it that the two of them found plenty of oppor-

Some youngsters act out their hostile feelings in violent fashion upon arriving at Monty's and must be controlled, to protect themselves as well as others.

TOM MC CARTHY, MIAMI

A schizophrenic child may try to hold on to some aspect of what is real to him by drawing zigzag lines on the classroom blackboard, filling in the spaces with the side of his chalk.

"When a little girl thinks she is a dog and will eat no other way than the way a dog eats," says Monty, "then this is the way we have to feed her."

Some children are so withdrawn that they have little patience even for play. They may remain in touch with their surroundings by peeking through their fingers now and then to see what is going on around them.

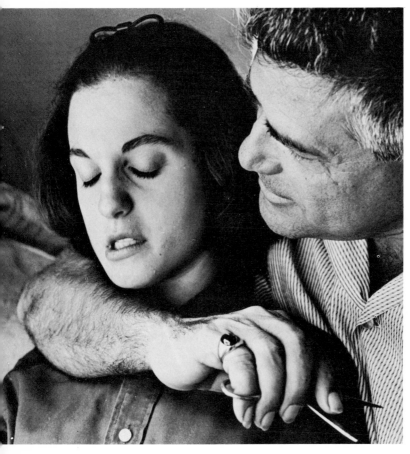

A terribly disturbed teenager might attempt to destroy herself in a moment of extreme anxiety. Such youngsters need the comfort of physical contact as well as understanding.

TOM MC CARTHY, MIAMI

A longing for home lies deep in every child but he cannot always express this feeling. When he becomes able to do so, it is often a sign that he is getting better.

Even the most severely disturbed children find it hard to resist reaching up to share the innocence that lies in Monty's hearty laughter and a bag of sweets.

tunity to get together. And that's what I told my staff: get them together but be subtle about it, don't let them know you're setting them up. Goddamnit, I was so excited about this thing I could hardly think of anything else."

It was difficult to create opportunities for Evelyn and Eugene to mix with one another, but a chance did arise one Saturday night when a room was cleared for a dancing party. To add to the festive atmosphere the room was decorated with balloons, paper lanterns and crayon sketches made by the children. Ruth and Jim Griffin, Alver and Miss Frances attended the party. So, of course, did Monty, who danced in a stumbling kind of way with the girls.

"Eugene was standing around, afraid to dance," recalls Monty. "So Ruth and Alver and Miss Frances went over to him and, well, they just made him go out on the floor and dance. Actually, he was a damn good dancer but he seemed to be afraid to approach a girl. So I began dancing with Evelyn, leading her over to where he was standing. Then I complained that I was beat and couldn't dance anymore. Looking straight at Eugene, I said, 'How about you taking over for me?' And right then and there, the two of them began to dance together and they stayed together the rest of the night."

When they weren't dancing, they were standing around together drinking Cokes. Monty or a staff member managed to approach unobtrusively from time to time to listen in on their conversation. At one point, Eugene was heard to say, "All adults are shit." Evelyn replied, with a smile, "You're right, all adults are shit."

They exchanged opinions about their families and Eugene seemed to be enjoying opportunities to make Evelyn laugh. Her laughter seemed to make him more sure of himself and more comfortable in her company.

On the following day, Evelyn seemed to be just a little bit more vivacious, more feminine, more genuinely excited about seeing Eugene in the yard after class. And once again they were overheard tearing apart their respective families. "I'd like to tell off my dirty old man one of these days," Evelyn said, and

Eugene remarked, "I'm getting awfully tired of making believe that I'm my mom's husband."

In so releasing their feelings to one another, they were indulging in a far healthier kind of rebellion than they had expressed before. And the more personal their exchange of feelings, the more inseparable they became. Soon they began to seek out one another, take walks together and, on occasion, hold hands. As their relationship deepened, they began to discard elements of their homosexual feelings.

Evelyn no longer spent hours gazing at her mirror. She looked at herself only long enough to apply a dab of makeup, comb her hair and arrange her dress so as to enhance her attractiveness as a female. Eugene no longer felt the need to express contempt for females and, before seeing Evelyn, took pains to see that his hair was properly combed. With him, as with her, there seemed to be a new excitement, as in their individual ways they explored their mutual dislikes, backgrounds and insecurities, and actively reached out for a common understanding.

The depth of their relationship was manifested by a tender little incident. Eugene was having his teeth straightened and, as part of his treatment, had to wear a "bite plate." One afternoon, following lunch, Eugene removed his bite plate, which was clogged with food, and Evelyn reached into her purse for a tissue with which to clean it. This small evidence of concern for his well-being seemed to have the effect of cementing their relationship.

"I suppose you might call them sweethearts," says Montanari, "but the only thing they ever did was to hold hands. They were pretty strange sweethearts, I guess, but they were pretty strange kids. I just don't know what would have happened to them if they hadn't discovered one another. I think they might have become homosexuals, because that's where they were heading."

It was their relationship that arrested their homosexual tendencies. Within a year, both were enrolled at the local Miami Springs High School, while they continued to live for several more months in residence.

After their discharge from Montanari's, they kept up a correspondence with one another for some time. Then they found new interests, healthy interests, and new friends.

"It would be nice," says Montanari, "if I could say that Evelyn and Eugene grew up and married one another. It would be a beautiful thing. But it didn't happen that way. As they became more adjusted socially, they began to date others. And, somehow, I think that's even more beautiful, considering what these kids have been through."

Montanari's success with these "strange sweethearts" served to pave the way for further expansion of the Clinical School and to prepare the way for an even more remarkable love story, that of Monty and his second wife.

VI

AFTER FIVE YEARS OF OPERATION, Montanari felt that he had
outgrown the one large house which sheltered the children and
the four greyhound kennels which served as classrooms. For, by
this time, both public and private agencies were pleading with
him to "take one more child."

But there was no room for more. There were not enough
paying customers to enable him to acquire new property. Only
a handful of parents paid the full fee of a hundred dollars a
month for day care and three hundred dollars a month for
residential care. More than half of the children were totally indigent and the wherewithal for their care was dependent on the
budget of the county welfare department and on the generosity
of the various agencies who placed youngsters with him.

"Somehow I managed to come up with the money to pay my
bills," Montanari says reflectively, "because I had to keep my
credit standing in the community. Without credit, I couldn't
go on. Sure, I needed more facilities but I couldn't afford them.
I wanted to hire some professional consultants and buy psychotherapy for the kids who might profit from it, but I couldn't
afford the twenty or twenty-five dollars an hour I had to pay,
and neither could these kids' folks or the agencies who sent them
to me. These doctors might work for nothing for an accredited
hospital, but not for me. The fact that they weren't working for
me, but for my kids, didn't seem to make much difference. So

we just went along, doing the best we could without professional help when we couldn't afford it."

Meanwhile, Montanari was beginning to attract the attention of out-of-state workers in the field. Notable among these was Dr. E. Paul Benoit, director of the Jewish Foundation for Retarded Children in Washington, D.C. Dr. Benoit visited the Clinical School several times, once as a representative of the American Psychiatric Association, and was impressed. "Here is abundant proof," he commented enthusiastically, "that although seriously disturbed children are difficult, they are not impossible. Mr. Montanari has demonstrated that these youngsters can be helped if we can only take away the irritations that have damaged them, and enable them to feel good about themselves and the world around them. This is a field which I believe strongly has been greatly handicapped by ineffective rationalization. Mr. Montanari has shown that with even limited facilities and resources he can bring healing and hope to these children and their troubled families. His school rose up like a miracle and this man is doing a tremendous job, treading where even the proverbial angels fear to tread."

It is interesting to note that, despite such encomiums, Montanari did not at that time—and still does not—qualify for financial support from either government or private-foundation sources. His record of accomplishment notwithstanding, he remains unaccredited. His is considered a private enterprise, not a nonprofit undertaking, although his yearly "profit" amounts to less than a truck driver's annual take-home pay. Ironically, if he were to alter his private status, he could multiply his income several times. For although the magic word "nonprofit" immediately conjures up visions of dedicated persons working selflessly on a near-subsistence level, the fact of the matter is that most nonprofit enterprises pay premium salaries to their directors, and generously support their fund-raising activities.

The Better Business Bureau, watchdog of the free-enterprise system, not infrequently levels a critical blast at various nonprofit, tax-free institutions for delegating as much as 90 percent of their income to fund-raising activities. Even the multimillion-dollar philanthropic foundations that lend financial support to so many worthwhile enterprises are not immune to criticism. The highly respected Ford Foundation has been reported by *The New York Times* as having received "repeated complaints that the foundation has grown too conservative, too sensitive to controversy and too much concerned with placing 'safe bets' on persons and institutions that are already successful." A host of extensive, expensive grants are made by a multitude of privately funded foundations, and by the federal government, drawing on public funds. But for Montanari's school, nothing.

"My kids are off limits to these handouts because I'm a private entrepreneur," Monty remarks without bitterness, but his mannerism of plucking at the corner of his lip with his thumb signals that his inner emotions are coming to a boil. "I have to go out and raise money in five- and ten-dollar dribbles from interested civic organizations, service groups and private citizens who aren't looking for a tax loophole. And every cent of it goes into my kids because mine is a child-centered institution. The child comes first. Everything is slanted to the child."

It is his contention that if he were to go "nonprofit," he would not be able to keep his costs down, not be able to extend his services to as many children and not be able to exercise his own judgment to the same extent in treating these children. He shakes his head in disbelief when informed that the Henry Ittleson Center for Child Research in New York has been endowed with almost half a million dollars for the construction of specially designed facilities for thirty-two emotionally disturbed children.

"God only knows how they're going to select the lucky thirty-two," he says. "But who's going to help the thousands of kids who aren't chosen, hm? I'd rather put that money into the kids and to hell with the fancy buildings."

Montanari breaks down the establishments that deal with troubled children into four basic categories. "One is what I would call staff-centered," he explains. "They worry about building up their professional staff and work on the premise that what's good for the staff is good for the child. I prefer to believe that what's good for the child is good for the staff. I don't pick my staff for administrative convenience. If one of my teachers has to hang around past her quitting time, she just stays there on the job. My people have never worked by the clock and I hope to God they never will, because disturbed kids don't control their feelings and their needs by the clock.

"Then there's what I call the research-centered institution. They have lots of money rolling in from all kinds of grants to try out this or that approach. Their kids are guinea pigs. Now, this is all right in a way because we have to look for new ways to get to these kids. But in my experience, most of this money goes down the drain because there are too many children who need some kind of help right now and they get lost in the shuffle of all this research.

"Then comes the socially centered setup where everything is geared to please the parents. The kids are put into fancy rooms, dressed up to look like real little ladies and gentlemen when their folks come around. But, goddamn it, these kids aren't little ladies and gentlemen. Why bother trying to impress the parents? It's not going to help the kids.

"Those institutions that concern themselves only with the children are what I call child-centered, same as my approach here. We don't attempt to have a child relate to any preconceived discipline. We look for a discipline that will relate to the individual child because no two children are the same. It seems to me that we're wasting a hell of a lot of time and talent and money searching for some perfect formula to heal these kids. I say, let's be less than perfect if we have to be, let's do it for less, but let's get started and just let's do the best we can for as many kids as we can in the shortest time possible."

Montanari leaves little doubt about the strength of his convictions. He does not play politics. He does not attempt to pacify those who can be helpful to him. If the political, economic and social tides run counter to a child's best interests, he hits the roof. "I don't want to go 'nonprofit,'" he says, "because I'd have to meet standards that I consider unrealistic. I'd have to raise my fees in order to hire a big staff of people with masters' degrees and PhD's in social work and psychology. Aside from the cost involved, where are you going to get such people? There aren't enough to go around. And, while you're waiting for them to graduate, who's going to help the kids meanwhile?"

His impatience is not without foundation. On a recent widely distributed television program backed by the New York State Citizens Committee for Mental Health, Dr. S. Mouchly Small, professor of psychiatry at Buffalo University, admitted, "In this metropolitan area with a population of over one and a half million, we have less than one psychiatrist for twenty-five thousand people and not a much greater proportion of psychologists and psychiatric social workers."

Dr. Alice Unger, a child psychiatrist, pointed out that the schools cannot cope with the increasing problems of emotional disturbance among children and that more and more parents come to the local child-guidance clinic only to be told that "the waiting list is fifty children long, which would mean a waiting period of at least three, four months or longer." She added that such a child would not need "a state hospital because he is not psychotic but he cannot be kept at home." The problem: no residential facilities available.

On the same program, Dr. Hugh Williams, a child psychiatrist, said, "We have a new children's unit at Meyer Memorial Hospital. That is, we have four walls of an eight-bed children's psychiatric unit. We don't have the beds. We don't have furniture or equipment. Most importantly, we don't have a staff to run a program for disturbed youngsters who might be treated here. A combination of not enough money for psychiatric service and too much red tape prevents us from assembling a psychiatric team to work here. I'm a child psychiatrist. I've been here since last August. That's eight months and I'm still trying to assemble a staff."

This is the essence of the dilemma which Montanari has chosen to avoid by doing things his own way. He is willing to overlook more highly specialized treatment on the premise that doing *something* is better than not doing anything at all. But despite his idealistic goals, his record of success and his devotion to the task which he had set for himself, he met with public resistance when he attempted to purchase five acres in South Miami in an effort to create an agricultural setting for about twenty teen-age boys who might profit emotionally, academically and vocationally from residential treatment in such surroundings.

"I had a chance to buy the property very reasonably, with almost no money down," Montanari recalls, "but the zoning board said no. The chief opposition came from homeowners who didn't want such a school in their neighborhood even though there was a chicken ranch in back of the property and a monkey jungle less than a mile away. They wanted me to move out into the swamps away from everybody. Well, hell, this was no good for my kids. They had to be in a residential area because this was part of their therapy. They had to get out into the community."

Montanari told the zoning board, "I just can't see why you can't raise children where you can raise chickens and monkeys!" And the local newspapers ate up the story, running headlines: "MONKEYS YES, CHILDREN NO."

Some insight into Montanari's highly emotional nature is suggested by Alver Louys, who recounts, "Monty was so mad about the ruling that he had to let off steam. He went into his office, closed the door and I could hear him muttering to himself in there. Suddenly, he began to kick the door and then he let out a yell. I rushed in and found that he had kicked the door so hard, he'd broken his toe. He took his disappointment out on himself, you see; that's his way of doing things. He makes himself suffer instead of somebody else."

"I guess I was frustrated," he explains, "because I couldn't find more space for kids who needed my services. So I kept looking around, figuring if I couldn't do it one way, I'd just do it another way, that's all."

On the corner of Second Street and East Third Avenue in Hialeah, a short block away from his school setting, stood a substantially constructed, spacious two-bedroom house owned by a neighborhood physician who had come to know Monty through attending some of the children. The physician no longer had need of the house and offered it to Montanari at a very low price, postponing the small down payment for another year.

"I grabbed at the opportunity," admits Monty. "It was a

good house, in a good section. I had to make a lot of changes, rip out walls, install a special kitchen and a lot of new equipment. This is something I have to do with all my property. I have to convert them into single-use dwellings because my kids need a very special kind of housing. But this house had plenty of grounds and there was room to expand, to build an extension for another classroom that would open right onto the big yard, and to put up a small office for myself where the kids could drop in whenever they wanted to talk to me."

He bought the property, eventually adding the extensions that he'd envisioned, but it required advance payments by two sets of parents to make the purchase and the necessary alterations. His benefactors proved to be two teen-age girls.

The first was Lucille, whose multiple physical ailments had resulted in emotional disturbance. At the age of four, Lucille had contracted spinal meningitis and suffered brain damage. At the age of ten, Lucille's problem was compounded by epilepsy. Her parents found her increasingly unmanageable and incorrigible and the family doctor advised drastic measures in an effort to correct Lucille's emotional insufficiency.

"She underwent surgery and a partial lobotomy, but it didn't help," her mother reveals. "My husband and I were panicky. We took her to some of the very best homes for disturbed children. But they all gave up on her. We had reached the point where we were ready to commit her to a state mental institution when a psychiatrist who had been treating her privately, but without success, suggested that we send her to Monty. Since there was no alternative, we decided to try. She remained with Monty almost two years. When she came back home, she wasn't the same girl anymore. Oh, she wasn't really a whole person; it's too late for that kind of miracle. But she was calmer, could do things for herself and was able to find small chunks of happiness here and there, something she could never do before. That was a good many years ago and she's still living at home with us. She makes her own bed, cleans up her room and does lots of things for herself. We love her and can show our love, and we feel pretty wonderful when she can throw her arms around us and tell us that she loves us, too. Because that was something she could never do before. And to a parent—I admit we're pretty selfish—this makes all the difference in the world."

Lucille's emotional difficulties arose from her organic disorders. "The doctors tried everything humanly possible," Montanari emphasizes, "but nothing helped. Besides a lobotomy, probably the most radical treatment of all, they tried shock therapy. Sometimes this works, sometimes it doesn't. Even when it does, nobody knows exactly why. I don't like it because it can destroy the memory cells of the brain. It's a shortcut to correcting emotional disturbance, but why take shortcuts with a child? I don't believe in cooking the brains out of a kid until you've tried everything else. I feel the same way about loading down a child with drugs. To me, this is committing chemical warfare on a youngster. I've seen too many doctors slow down kids with drugs just to keep them from raising hell and make them easier to work with. This may be good for the doctors, but what about the child? I think someday the biochemists are going to come up with medication that will really cut through the fog of a troubled child but, even then, reeducation will have to come from another human being, not from a hypodermic needle. With Lucille, they went all the way and nothing helped. She had to be carefully supervised, and subtly retrained. We had to make her understand that she wasn't a monster, just a sick little girl, but that we loved her just the same. It was too late for psychoanalysis or psychotherapy. She couldn't be reached that way. Some kids, you know, are either too sick or too well for such treatment to be effective. When they're too sick, they can't be reached. And when they're too well, they don't want to be reached. I've found that most disturbed kids fall between these categories and, for them, the nonclinical approach seems to work best."

The other teen-ager whose advance tuition benefited Montanari was a tall, strikingly pretty, dark-haired girl named Karen. She was the second-born of three children and had been raised in a happy, loving family. Like Lucille, her organic problems triggered her emotional difficulties. But her organic problems differed in many ways and Karen had not been subjected to the same radical treatment. Montanari's own interest in working with her was, in fact, enhanced by the knowledge that Karen had not had extensive contact with others in the field.

"Karen was born with a congenital heart defect," says her mother, a woman of great charm and beauty. Her frequent and infectious smile seems to be an attempt to disguise the real depth of her feelings, for it is plain that this is a woman of great sensitivity. "It took years before the doctors realized that Karen had been born brain-damaged as well. It showed up first in her lack of physical coordination. Then she became unduly temperamental, unpredictable in her behavior. Her older brother, Herbert, and her younger sister, Joyce, had to go out of their way to be considerate of Karen. If she did not approve of something, our family changed its plans. In looking back, I must confess that raising Karen was harder than raising ten other children. Her heart defect prevented her from getting about and her brain impairment prevented her from advancing herself either intellectually or emotionally. It was a terrible thing for us to accept, but we just had no alternative."

Karen's mother, then Mrs. Carol Straus, became widowed when her family was still very young. Fortunately, she was left in comfortable circumstances. Since Karen was unable to attend public school, or even private school, because of her frequent seizures, her mother was forced to engage a private tutor.

"Her tutor," Mrs. Bertha Newhall, a wonderfully patient woman," her mother recalls, "was of great help to Karen. When the child threw one of her terrible tantrums, this woman knew just how to console her. She became a substitute for the friends whom Karen could not seem to make, and she managed to teach Karen to read, to write and to make the most of her few blessings. When this woman became ill and had to leave, Karen became distraught and I did, too. Our family physician advised me to place her in a residential center for emotionally disturbed children. Well, I did, against my better judgment. I placed her for one summer in a well-known residential school in the East, but it just didn't work out. I was never permitted to visit her without making an appointment well in advance and this annoyed me and made me suspicious.

"When I first saw the room they assigned to her—neatly

decorated with organdy curtains, pretty pictures and all sorts of little dolls and things—I knew that Karen could not be comfortable there. For this wasn't her. She wasn't neat. She couldn't be neat. They were asking too much of her and I could imagine that she was tearing the place apart, and that they were slapping her hands for messing things up. So I took her out of the school and moved my family to Miami, just to get away from New York and all the old memories. I had the crazy thought that maybe the warm climate would have a soothing effect on Karen, for she was becoming harder and harder to manage."

From a copy of the *Miami News,* Karen's mother clipped a story about the Montanari Clinical School, but could not make up her mind to take the child there. When Karen experienced increasing difficulty in getting along with other children and became even more explosive, Mrs. Straus telephoned a cousin who lived in Miami and said that something had to be done because Karen's behavior was beginning to have a bad effect on the other children.

"It must have been fate," she recalls happily, "because my cousin Marian said she had just been listening to a man named Montanari on the local radio station and that this man ran a different kind of school for severely disturbed children. She thought that his place sounded just right for Karen. Well, the name rang a bell in my mind. I remembered the story in the *Miami News,* and right then and there I telephoned Mr. Montanari for an appointment."

She recalls that she was immediately impressed by the unpretentious country setting. "It looked homey," she says. "There was a big collie dog with a litter of pups out on the front lawn and there were children everywhere playing under the supervision of several grownups. I remember how Karen's eyes lit up when she saw the place and I remember praying to myself that it would really turn out to be everything it seemed to be, a place where my daughter could have room to run about, to play, to make friends and to overcome some of her difficulties."

Karen's mother recalls that even as she walked toward Monty's office, she began to sense that the children who seemed to be playing so innocently were not at all ordinary. They were, in the most misleading euphemism of our time, "exceptional" children. One little girl walked up to her and said, laughingly, "Hiya, alligator," then gave her a bone-crushing hug and remarked, "You feel like a box of cotton, nice and soft, and I love you." A small boy strutted over to her, grinned, then quite suddenly sat down in her path. He began to rock back and forth violently, clutching his knees to his chest, and murmuring over and over, "You've come for me, Mother, you've come for me, Mother, you've come for me . . ." And a girl of Karen's age ran beside her, waving a pencil and a sheaf of papers in her hand, saying over and over, "I have to reduce my notes, I have to reduce them to intelligibility," and then, quite suddenly, she seated herself beside a large flat rock to write feverishly upon a fresh sheet of paper.

"It was shocking," Mrs. Straus recalls, "but these children did not frighten me. I had become so accustomed to Karen's bizarre behavior that I actually felt comfortable with them. I suppose Karen did, too, because she didn't seem to cling quite so tightly to my arm and she kept smiling at these children, perhaps finding in them a kindred spirit."

When she met Monty in his tiny office that held only a battered old desk and two broken-down chairs, she was surprised to find him attired in a sport shirt and wrinkled slacks. "He had none of that professional look to which I had become accustomed," she says, laughing. "He was different, too, because he paid practically no attention to me at all, only to Karen. She quite suddenly began to cry, to scream, and I remember she punched him when he approached her. I warned him then, 'Mr. Montanari, my daughter is going to tear up your books, everything in your office, and you might as well know it.' Well, he just grinned and put his arm around her firmly, saying, 'Mrs. Straus, Karen and I are going to take a little walk together. You look the place over in the meantime.' He didn't even wait for me to answer, just walked out with Karen. I was too stunned to say a word. I walked around the place and about fifteen minutes later, when I came back to the office, Monty returned with Karen. She was calm, smiling and holding tightly to his hand. I was absolutely astonished. I just couldn't figure it out."

In recalling the incident, Montanari says, modestly, "What did I do? What had I really done? I became a friend of this child, that's all. I let her know that I wasn't afraid of anything she might do and that she was no different from any of my other friends. I walked with her, I talked to her, I took her on a tour of the place and had her meet my other kids. Then I brought her back to her mama. That's all I did."

In such understatement lies the "magic" of Montanari, the essence of his ability to "charm children," as Dr. Tousseing of the Menninger Clinic has termed it. When Karen was put into his charge, first as a day student and later as a residential student, he said to her mother, "You are not paying me to take care of Karen, but to train her to get along with herself and with life. I don't intend to be her custodian. I want to be her teacher."

But before he would attempt to reeducate Karen, emotionally or intellectually, he insisted on having her examined physically. "I do this with all my kids," he explains, "but with Karen it was especially important because of her heart condition. Frankly, I felt that she had been overprotected. She'd been forced to rest after every meal for two hours. Well, I had once learned from a doctor friend of mine that youngsters who were cardiac cases from birth were their own best thermometers. So I got the OK of the physician who examined Karen, took her for walks with me and put a stop to those compulsory rest periods. When she got tired, and had to squat down to rest, we rested. When it was too much for her to continue, I took her back to the school on my shoulders piggy-back. It was fun for her and turned out to be good for her heart. I continued to have the doctor check her out and after a while he told me that her heart seemed stronger. She began to feel less and less tired. Today she can go, go, go without ever bothering to rest."

This improvement in her physical stamina seemed to build up her ego appreciably. The tradition of "payday" also had a beneficial effect on Karen, her house mother, Miss Frances, recalls: "Every Friday, Monty hands an envelope to each child with his or her name on it. Inside is that child's weekly allowance. It might be fifty cents, or a dollar, even more if the child merits a reward by doing something extra—helping to look after a younger child, mimeographing a little newspaper for everyone to read or doing a bit of painting. Karen just loved to get this envelope with her name on it. Somehow, it made her feel important and she enjoyed planning how to spend her allowance."

But Karen was not easy to manage. Ruth Griffin, who was then the school's principal, remembers, "Karen often became very angry and would pull off her shoes and throw them at whoever annoyed her. If you didn't duck fast, you could really be hurt. When she wasn't being aggressive, she was very withdrawn. Then she would sit for hours by herself unraveling the elastic webbing in a girdle or a cushion, and it was almost impossible to distract her at those times."

Alver Louys, who was her teacher, adds, "She was very sensitive to criticism. If another child whispered something nasty into her ear, she was likely to blow up and throw an awful tantrum. It was a problem because these disturbed kids have a devilish ability to pick out the sore spots in other children. We have to be on our toes for this sort of thing because, when it happens, it's liable to start off a chain reaction."

She relates how such a chain reaction took place one evening after an all-day rain. It became apparent that the children were becoming restless. Staff members were muttering to one another, "This rain is keeping the kids on edge. We're in for an explosion." Alerted to the danger, they used every resource to keep the children occupied.

The tension mounted as darkness began to settle over the tops of the palm trees lining the streets. None of the staff went home. They stayed, watching, waiting, encouraging the children to laugh, to play or to pass the time by watching the rain.

As always, at such times, Monty paced about from one dormitory to another, seeking out subtle signs of discontent among his charges, murmuring admonitions to his staff to "watch Diane over there, she's getting moody," and "better separate Andy from the other boys and play dominoes with him; he looks ready to blow up."

He came to Karen's dormitory, accompanied by Ruth Griffin. In a low voice, he discussed some of the new arrivals with Miss

Frances, the house mother, and Alver, who was staying on until the girls were tucked into bed and sleeping. He greeted the girls quietly to avoid the possibility of any undue stimulation, exchanged glances with Miss Frances and Alver and received reassuring nods in return. So far, all was well.

Seated unobtrusively in a corner, not far from where Karen sat brushing her hair, was Jean, a statuesque, pimple-faced girl who was sometimes described as "having no countenance" because she would sit transfixed, staring into space, for hours on end.

Squatting on the floor in the middle of the room was chubby Vivian, who giggled foolishly to herself every now and then. And behind her was Barbara, a wide-eyed little girl with curly blond hair who was subject to auditory hallucinations. A severe traumatic shock when she was eleven years old had resulted in her hearing voices from "a man in my head who tells me I'm a bad, bad girl." The accusations of this imaginary man invariably drove her into a shrieking frenzy.

The girls seemed to be at peace, so, after a few minutes, Monty started to leave. Just as he was closing the door behind him, he froze, exclaiming, "Oh, God, here it comes!"

Too late, he had spotted Jean suddenly turning, putting her lips to Karen's ear and hissing. Frightened, Karen leaped up, flung the mirror and hairbrush across the room and began to scream uncontrollably. This stimulated Vivian to race frantically about the room, giggling hysterically. The cacophony unloosed by the hair-triggered emotions of her roommates grated on the raw nerves of Barbara, who became bewildered and felt intimidated. Clapping her hands to her ears, she raised her voice in a shrill unearthly wail: "He's coming, he's coming, the man in my head . . . no, no, no!"

It all happened within seconds. One oversensitive nerve touched off another. Suddenly the room became an echo chamber of fierce yells and foolish laughter.

But with the same kind of quickness that had set off this chain reaction, the staff responded. "Ruth Griffin went to Barbara, who was nearest to her," recounts Alver, "holding her close to restrain her from beating her head against the wall. Miss Frances rushed over to Vivian and shook her, speaking to her firmly to put a stop to her hysterical giggling. I grabbed Jean, who'd started the whole thing, and drew her aside, away from the others. Monty went to Karen and tried to soothe her while she kept screaming in his ears. It seemed like hours but it only took about five minutes before we had them all quieted down again. Then the girls just sat around as if nothing had happened. Monty was a mess. His face was all scratched up and bleeding from Karen's fingernails. He left and we put the girls to bed. They went right to sleep and then I went home."

In the anecdotal records kept by the staff, this highly dramatic incident is entered simply: "Chain reaction in the girls' cottage. Cause: the all-day rain. Uneventful. The girls went to bed nicely."

This casual attitude is an integral part of day-to-day practice at the Clinical School. The drama suggested by such incidents impresses only the outsider. To the staff they are considered routine, part of the job. Monty did not even bother to mention the incident to Karen's mother.

"It wasn't important," he says with a careless shrug of his shoulders. "It would only upset her, so why bother talking about it? Karen wasn't any worse for it. She had more urgent problems that had to be taken care of."

Occasions arose when Karen would get convulsive seizures and be unable to attend class. Her pediatrician was consulted and he changed her medication from Dilantin to Mysoline (an anti-convulsive drug) and it seemed to work. "Knock wood, she had no further seizures after that," says Monty. "But I still looked upon this kind of medication as just a temporary measure and was trying to bring Karen around to the point where she could function without medication of any kind."

The basic therapy consisted of long walks and long talks with Monty, who soon became the second most important person in Karen's life. When she became troubled, she turned first to her mother and then to Monty for affection and understanding. She was a demanding child and Monty was able to meet her demands more firmly than her mother, since he was not tied to her with the same kind of emotional bond. So when, for example, Karen would demand a record to play on the phonograph in her cottage and it was not forthcoming, Monty would respond to her annoyance by saying, "Karen, I know that you told me you *wanted* this record, but I didn't say that I would *give* it to you. I might like to let you have the record, and maybe I will, but you can't have it just because you insist upon it, do you understand that, honey? Do you understand that you just can't always have what you want?"

He was attempting to raise the child's tolerance for frustration, something her mother could not do because she would consider it cruel. As an outsider, Monty considered it realistic and imperative to Karen's future well-being.

Despite his divorce, his children were frequent visitors to the school and they enjoyed mingling with the children. His daughter, Cissy, a bright and pretty little girl, was younger than Karen but was able to relate to her. Whenever she visited, she sought Karen out and helped to build Karen's faith in herself to the point where she could interact easily with other girls.

Monty's interest in Karen, however, ran even deeper than he suspected. Almost every day he would telephone Mrs. Straus to apprise her of her daughter's progress. "Today I gave Karen a manicure because she picked at her cuticles," he would tell her proudly. A number of times he accepted her mother's invitation to bring some of his children to her home on Indian Creek in Miami where they could swim from the dock behind her home. At such times, Karen's mother would prepare lunch for the youngsters and both she and Monty would derive great pleasure from these get-togethers. It did not occur to either of them that, through Karen, they were beginning to express interest in one another until a trick of fate threw them together in a somewhat different setting.

Karen's mother was eager to learn all that she could about emotionally disturbed children and frequently attended public meetings on the subject. One evening, she and her cousin attended such a meeting at a local auditorium. The guest speaker happened to be A. J. Montanari. From the speaker's platform, Monty noticed her in the audience and, at the termination of his talk, went directly over to her to ask if she and her cousin would join him and his guest, Dr. Benjamin A. Stevens, for a drink.

"My cousin and I accepted Mr. Montanari's invitation for a drink," says Karen's mother, unable to repress a broad grin, "and where do you think he took us? To an orange-drink stand just down the street! Then he drove us home in his dinky old second-hand car."

But it marked the beginning of a new and closer relationship. Monty began to stop at the home of Karen's mother on the pretext of discussing Karen. She began to look forward to his visits and says, "Our relationship developed so gradually that it just seemed so natural, so inevitable. At first we talked only about Karen. Then we talked about my other children and about Monty's children. And pretty soon, little by little, we began to find more and more in common."

Montanari is a sentimental man and his ways of wooing appear to be equally sentimental. He admits frankly, "One night I called on Carol with no other intention than to tell her about Karen's progress. She had to go to the drugstore for some things and I offered to drive her there. Well, when I was taking her back home, I suddenly found myself driving with one hand and holding Carol's hand with the other. I didn't plan it that way, it just seemed to happen, that's all."

He relates the story with a self-conscious grin that reminds the observer of an overgrown schoolboy. Here, perhaps, is further insight into the man and the remarkably rare kind of honesty that enables him to relate so tangibly to children. Such a courtship might be laughed off by some as "square," but before Monty and Carol could arrive at the point where they were ready to exchange vows of love, they had reached deeply into each other's hearts. The catalyst was Karen. Through their mutual concern for the child, they discovered their affection for one another.

By any standards, this is a strange romance. Carol is Jewish and Monty Italian. But since he has never been truly committed to any religious affiliation, he felt quite comfortable worshiping God in Carol's temple. He got on splendidly with her rabbi, who blessed their union and signed their marriage license in mid-November of 1958.

"I was uncomfortable only because I was still struggling to make a living," Monty confesses. "Carol had known better times and I felt I might be jumping up too high. But I talked it out with her and she agreed that we'd just have to live on my level."

"We were quite frank with each other," Carol adds. "I knew how he was still fighting to establish himself and that I'd known better circumstances than he could provide. But I saw what he had done for Karen and other children, and this meant a great deal to me. I believed in this man and the work he was doing and I think he needed this kind of faith from me to keep him going. His work meant that much to him."

In many ways, it was a picture-book romance. After the marriage ceremony, Monty brought Carol to Winchendon, Massachusetts, to visit his family. She came laden down with numerous brown paper bags containing lox and bagels purchased in Miami. They were met at the airport by Monty's sister, Hilda, her husband, Dave Bartlett, and their children, Chip and Jane. Then they drove together to the home of Monty's father and mother. Here, their cultures merged in good-natured fashion, as they commenced the family dinner with lox and bagels and then proceeded to such Italian delicacies as ravioli and veal parmigiana prepared by Monty's mother. Plenty of home-brewed red wine, lots of laughter and a great store of sentimental reminiscences added to the festivities and set the style for future family get-togethers.

As for Karen, she has never been able to reach the point of complete self-sufficiency. She has been too damaged. But she has made many friends at the Clinical School and often says to her mother after dinner, "I want to sleep home tonight with my friends." For she considers her dormitory at the school no less her "home" than the private room at her own house. At the former, she has her teachers, house parents and girlfriends, to whom she relates in good, healthy fashion, while at the latter, she has her family, which now includes her stepbrother, Gary, who has come to live with his father.

"You have to look at things philosophically," says Carol Montanari with a wistful smile. "In many ways, Karen is a lot luckier than most other girls. She has two homes where she is wanted and welcome."

Monty may be sentimental, but when it comes down to the brass tacks of obtaining assistance for troubled kids, sentiment yields to a canny business sense that brings out the "wheeler-dealer" in him. Not long after his marriage to Carol, he became acquainted with Henry Milander, the long-time mayor of Hialeah as well as the owner of the city's leading meat market. Mayor Milander had a house adjacent to Montanari's property which he offered to sell him for only $8,000.

With an ingenuity born of desperation, Monty withdrew his last $500 from the bank and used it as a temporary down payment. He then talked the local bank into letting him have a first mortgage of $8,500, promising to spend $6,000 to improve the property. Then, on the strength of his personal reputation, he fast-talked his way into a $6,000 personal loan from another bank. On the same day, he turned the $6,000 over to a contractor, who agreed to make the necessary renovations. Armed with the contractor's acceptance of this agreement, he rushed back to the first bank and completed the loan for $8,500. After paying $8,000 of this to the mayor, he was left with $500, the amount of his original investment, which he used as operating expenses.

He was growing now, becoming more entrenched in the community. Soon he was sent a small boy who became one of his most challenging cases. "He is a 'vegetable,' unable to respond to even the most primitive demands of life," the referring physician told him sadly. "I'm afraid it's just a waste of time sending him to you because he really belongs in an institution. He's hopeless. He's just a 'potato.'" And this small boy whose name was Paul became known from that moment on as "Paul the Potato."

VII

PAUL HARRIS WAS FIVE AND A HALF but weighed no more than a three-year-old and related to his surroundings no better than a one-year-old. He slept in a crib, drank milk from a bottle and still wore diapers because he defecated in his pants. He spoke no words, made only grunting sounds, and cried constantly. His only physical activities were rocking back and forth in his crib and squatting limply on the floor, waving his fingers about in the air. Doctors classified him as "severely retarded."

None could accurately pinpoint the basic cause of Paul's startling lack of maturation but a variety of reasons were suggested. As an infant, Paul was almost inert, unable to smile or respond in any way to either parent. In his first year, he fell out of his crib and struck his head on the hardwood floor. During his infancy, he suffered an unusual number of illnesses ranging from measles to whooping cough, and much of the time he was entrusted to the care of a maid, who was discovered later to have been shockingly indifferent to the child's needs.

In discussing the case, Montanari says, "Paul was a very appealing little boy despite all his troubles. I took a look at him and thought to myself, 'My God, Monty, how can you let this boy be institutionalized for the rest of his life? He's too young to be written off as a vegetable.' I had the feeling that his lack of development was the result of his emotional difficulties and that his abilities were dormant. Mental retardation, after all, is something we know very little about, even today."

Paul's parents surrendered their son to Montanari with misgivings. "We had a lovely home in New England that we gave up to move here," confides Mrs. Harris. "Monty's place seemed so barren in comparison. And when we saw the sick children with whom Paul would have to live, we could hardly bring ourselves to let him go."

"If it wasn't that we took such a liking to Monty," adds Mr. Harris, "I wouldn't have let Paul go."

Montanari recalls the incident with a wry smile. "There was an awful to-do when the Harrises said good-bye to Paul," he says. "Mrs. Harris was crying hysterically and Mr. Harris was just as bad. But they had no choice. Nobody else would take their son. If I didn't, they'd have to put him away someplace. Or they'd have to go on keeping him home, which wasn't doing any of them any good. They'd become so overprotective that they were making their child more and more dependent. As for my having him live with other sick children, well, that's therapy in itself. I don't say this is where the good kids are; this is where the bad kids are. All of them are God's children and, in living together, they help each other. But it's pretty hard to make a concerned parent see things that way."

Paul was enrolled on a three-month trial basis, a standard practice at the Clinical School. The first step in Paul's treatment was his removal from a crib to a bed. The child screamed in protest and Monty was forced to sit beside his bed for many nights, but he considered it important in the upgrading of Paul's behavior and emotional attitude.

The second step was toilet-training. "If a child is not toilet-trained," Monty contends, "there is a big line drawn between him and other children. Every time he urinates on the floor or defecates in his pants, he emphasizes the difference between himself and others. His freedom becomes restricted and he limits his social progress. But once he has been toilet-trained, we can pull him into another area of living, get him out more—into the classroom, into the shop, into town—and help him to relate better to other kids."

Parents commonly train their offspring by placing them on the toilet at certain times each day and encouraging them to eliminate. Montanari reversed this procedure. He discovered that youngsters like Paul tended to soil their pants *after* being removed from the toilet. So, instead, he brought such youngsters to the toilet *after* soiling and very casually encouraged them to sit there, for about ten minutes, until elimination was *completed*. Thus did he attempt to establish in a positive nonpunitive way a reasonable association between being on the toilet and eliminating.

Within two weeks, Paul became sufficiently reliable to have his diapers removed. Within two more weeks, he was soiling very infrequently and taking pride in going to the bathroom by himself. His pride soon increased to the point where he would take Monty, a staff member, or even a visitor by the hand and lead them to the bathroom to show off the results of his training.

Paul continued to rock back and forth in his bed or on his heels while squatting on the ground. This is a habit common to emotionally disturbed youngsters. In an attempt to counteract such habits, Montanari purchased a large rocking horse and set it out in the play yard. He encouraged other children to climb upon it and to rock back and forth where Paul could see them. When the child giggled as he rocked on the horse, Monty laughed with him, subtly trying to elicit Paul's curiosity.

After several days had gone by, Monty sensed that Paul was ready for the new experience. Disregarding the boy's cries, he placed him on the horse, while holding him protectively around the waist. Vigorously, Monty forced the horse to rock back and forth. Paul's objections gradually subsided and he began to move with the horse. Within a few weeks, he ceased to rock in bed or while squatting on the ground and, instead, clambered up on the rocking horse.

Weaning Paul away from the bottle proved more difficult. It required a month of patient, disappointing trials before he would even allow himself to be fed from a cup. When he finally decided to do so, he insisted on standing while Monty or one of the staff fed him from the cup. It was, however, the presence of other children which finally convinced Paul to drink from a cup.

"Paul's companions used to coax him to sit down at the table with them," comments Montanari, "and pretty soon he did just that. You see, he wanted to be like the other kids. He wanted to feel he was part of the crowd. This is what I mean when I say that a disturbed child can learn from other kids. They get emotional support from each other."

Two months went by. Paul still could not speak intelligibly. He continued to form sounds—high-pitched whines when frustrated, low humming from deep in his throat when content—but he could not make words from the sounds, and this became a matter of great concern to Montanari.

"He had to learn to express himself in words in order to convey his feelings to me and my staff," Monty explains. "He had to learn to use words as a means of self-protection. It was the only way he could let us know when another child was bugging him, the only way he could tell us he wanted something. But he had to be motivated to learn before we could try to teach him. So we waited until his frustration at not being able to express himself became overwhelming. Then we started teaching him."

Monty was Paul's first teacher but, as usual, he did not confine his teaching to the classroom. He took Paul outdoors and for walks in the community.

When the boy seemed ready to learn speech, Monty first taught him to imitate vowel sounds, for these were most closely related to the sounds he made habitually. When Paul had mastered vowels, Monty taught him how to form the more difficult consonant sounds. He introduced him, first, to fundamental words like "me," "you," "boy," "girl," "eat," "sleep," and so on. Later, pointing to a robin in the grass, he would repeat, over and over again, "Bird . . . that is a bird, Paul . . . bird . . . look at that bird . . . that is a bird, bird, bird."

Gradually, after many, many hours of work Paul began to form intelligible words and to show interest in enlarging his slim vocabulary. One very hot afternoon, Monty lifted Paul high over his head, making the child squeal with happy excitement. Putting him down, Monty mopped his brow. "I'm too hot to play anymore," he said with a wide grin. "I'm too hot."

Paul looked up at him and grinned back, repeating, "Too hot, you too hot."

Monty laughs as he recollects the incident. "For a long while after that," he says, "Paul used to yell out, every time he saw me, 'Hello, Too Hot!' That's what he called me—'Too Hot.'"

By the time the three-month trial period was over, Montanari felt assured that Paul was well on the way. He had the boy re-evaluated at the psychological institute of Jackson Memorial Hospital, part of the Miami University School of Medicine, and the report was favorable: "The patient has improved considerably . . . plays more with other children . . . participates more in group activities."

Until this time, Montanari had discouraged Mr. and Mrs. Harris from visiting Paul. "It's very important for kids to go home on weekends, or at least to have their folks visit them," he explains, "but sometimes parents can upset a child and create more problems than they resolve. This was the case with Paul's parents. On their first visit, they became so emotional that they only succeeded in making things tougher for their son. So I told them they would have to stay away until I felt that Paul was ready to see them. I spoke to them frequently by telephone and wrote them letters to reassure them."

Montanari's letters were informal, casual and personal. Typical is the following, written about two months after Paul entered the school:

DEAR STEVE AND MABEL,
Paul is getting along just fine so stop worrying. Go on that vacation you've planned and let us do the worrying. That's what you're paying us for. I promise you that we'll look after him affectionately because we love him just as you do. It will do you both good to get away for a few days. Have a good time and give me a ring when you get back.
                                                                MONTY

It was almost four months before Montanari felt that Paul had reached a point in his redevelopment where a weekend visit home would be beneficial to his progress. When Ruth Griffin surrendered Paul to his parents, she told them, "Your son may be extremely demanding at this stage and very upsetting to you. But if you can't handle him, please don't fuss with him. Just put him in the car and drive him back to us. Let *us* handle him."

Paul adjusted quite well to his first visit home and his parents were astonished by his progress. "For the first time in his life," Mrs. Harris says, "he actually talked. He called me 'Mom' and he called his father 'Dad.' It's hard to explain how much this meant to us."

Alver Louys was Paul's next teacher. She taught him to tie his own shoelaces, a remarkable achievement for such a disturbed youngster. She also taught him to write letters by guiding the pencil in his hand, and to identify colors by using color cards and a bit of subterfuge.

"When I asked him to match the correct color name with the proper color card," she explains, "I excluded the purple and brown cards, but gave him the *names* of those colors to see what his reaction would be. Well, when he came to these names and couldn't find the matching cards, he paused, said 'Uh-oh,' then went ahead. After he was all through, he turned to me and said, 'The purple and brown color cards are missing.' I got so excited I just couldn't stop hugging him!"

Commenting on the attitude of his staff, Montanari says, "Oh, God, they were wonderful. They took him home lots of times, the same as I did, to see how he got along in a family setting. And if they saw him running off to hide behind a tree, or in a closet, they stayed around long after it was time for them to go home, trying to lure him back from his hiding place."

Monty wrote many memos to his staff about Paul. One, to Mrs. Louys, reads: "Keep on with what you are doing in the classroom but don't cuddle him too much because he might revert to clinging again. Give him things to hold, things to do. Limit your attention carefully so that he can develop perception of others and feel that he is part of the group." Another, to a house mother, reads: "Stop feeding him only the food he likes. He must learn to eat a varied diet. It won't hurt him to miss two or even three meals in a row, if necessary, to get this point across. Eventually he'll become hungry enough to eat whatever is set before him. Invite him to eat what is served but don't push him too hard. If he is reluctant to join the group, set his plate at a table by himself. Don't push him, take it easy."

Alver Louys tells an illuminating anecdote about Monty's reaction to Paul and the other children in his care. "One day," she says, "Monty was all dressed up, on the way to an important luncheon meeting in town. He had on a clean white shirt and the clip-on bowtie he always wears when he goes out. Well, as he was walking through the yard, Paul and a couple of other kids ran over to him. They were all pretty sloppy, full of jam and marmalade from breakfast and lots of healthy dirt from playing in the yard. They jumped all over Monty, demanding to be hugged, and he didn't say, 'I'll hug you later, don't dirty me up.' Full of smiles, he hugged them right back and then just walked back to the house, changed his shirt, clipped on a fresh bowtie and went out again. He was late for his luncheon meeting but that didn't bother him a bit. That's the way he is. His kids come first."

This kind of attention helped to reinforce Paul's social attitude. Montanari placed great importance on it because he felt that the boy's capacity for academic learning would increase in direct proportion to his social gains.

Paul had begun to find his own identity and do things for himself. He could open and close the windows of his room and turn on the drinking fountain without assistance. But he had become egocentric to the point where he could not distinguish between the concepts of "yours" and "mine." He would, for example, say to his teacher, "Please lock up my books so the other boys won't get even one dirty fingerprint on them." Having learned to respect himself, he despised others.

Gradually, as he became more self-assured, his resistance to his classmates gave way to a more carefree "who cares" kind of attitude. With increased social awareness, he demonstrated interest in the rights of others. He began to find pleasure in holding the drinking fountain for his less fortunate classmates, in sharing his possessions, and he even went so far as to mop up puddles on the floor that were made by the smaller children at the school.

"In modern society," says Montanari, "a child has to learn to get along with everybody else. He has to learn to take his place in line at the bus, at the movies, at the cafeteria. It was important for Paul to learn to do this, to learn how to put up with frustration, to understand the other fellow's needs and, at the same time, to be able to stand up for his own rights."

When Paul reached his seventh year, a party was thrown in his honor. Mr. and Mrs. Harris were invited and were delighted to see how their son, after blowing out the candles on his birthday cake, waited patiently for all the guests to be served before reaching for his own slice of birthday cake.

"It was hard to believe that this was the same boy who had come to Monty's school only a year and a half before," Mrs. Harris remarks. "My husband and I felt like real parents for the first time."

As Paul's social awareness increased, his capacity to absorb intellectual training increased as well. He was far behind his grade level but, Montanari points out, "He moved ahead faster than anyone else in his class."

Paul remained in residence for three years—twice as long as the average child—and continued for another year as a day student. When he was discharged, Mr. and Mrs. Harris enrolled him in a private school where he could receive special attention. Fortunately for Paul, his parents were in a position to afford the expense.

Slowly, methodically, he caught up on his schoolwork to the point where he is presently only a single year behind his grade level. He has won a number of honors for scholastic achievement and is described by his teachers as "a perfectionist, pleasant, cooperative and ambitious."

Quite often, he drops in on Monty unannounced. On a recent visit, Paul admitted, "I was awfully glad to leave this place and go back home. But every once in a while I like to come back and see Monty because he is one of my very best friends."

Interestingly enough, Paul remains in contact with only one other child from the school, a boy who was in no way like him and who had not been blessed with devoted parents. On the contrary, this youngster was a welfare case, abandoned by his parents, and at the age of five he had murdered his baby sister.

For this reason, Jimmy Wilson made headlines as "the five-year-old killer."

Social workers who laboriously pieced together the details of Jimmy's early existence refer to the boy as "a classic example of the effects of emotional deprivation." Their findings indicate that Jimmy's mother was an unstable, anxiety-ridden woman and his father a hard-drinking, harsh disciplinarian who scraped together a meager livelihood working at a variety of menial chores. The family lived in a decrepit shack in the Florida swamps. Both parents were religious fanatics who instilled in their son the terrors of hell—but not the love of God.

For the first three years of his life, Jimmy struggled for laughter but his demonstrations of boyish mischief were met with scowls and beatings and threats of perdition. The result of this harsh attitude was to infect the mischief and poison the pranks.

Jimmy had a baby sister and became terribly jealous of any attention paid to her by his parents. When she crept across the bare wood floor of the kitchen for the first time, he saw his mother hug the little girl and shout happily, "Sarah's crawling!"

This made him furious and, instinctively, he seized his toy shovel and smashed it down across his sister's back. His father lunged for him, screaming, "You'll go to hell for that!" and beat Jimmy black and blue.

This only served to make Jimmy angrier. He sought further opportunities to attack Sarah. One day, Mr. and Mrs. Wilson found Jimmy in Sarah's playpen, chewing on her ears and clawing at her face with his fingernails. They beat him and cursed him, and were so enraged that they reported his behavior to the local authorities.

"There is nothing we can do," the Wilsons were informed. "We can't put the boy in jail. If he had TB or polio, we could put him in the hospital, but he isn't sick. He's just a wild kid."

To protect Sarah, they moved her bed into their room and let Jimmy have his room to himself. They tried to discipline the boy by reminding him, at the slightest evidence of misbehavior, that he was a sinner and would be punished by God.

Soon after Jimmy reached the age of five, another girl was

born to the family. A neighbor reported that Jimmy was very upset by this new addition and had remarked, "God is punishin' me because he knows I don't want no more sisters around."

Since there wasn't space enough in the Wilson's bedroom to accommodate two children, Jimmy was forced to give up his room to Sarah and his new baby sister. He now had to sleep in a cot alongside his parents' bed.

"Of course, this made Jimmy hate his sisters even more," Montanari explains, "but nobody suspected just how deep that hatred went. One night, he sneaked out of bed and stole into his old room, where his sisters were sleeping. He was only five and a half years old at the time but clever enough with his hands to unscrew the valve of an old gas heater. Having done this, he crept out, closing the door behind him and went back to bed. By morning, the baby was dead and Sarah was alive only by a miracle."

Jimmy later told a psychologist, "I didn't mean to kill 'er, honest, I jist meant to scare 'em, that's all." He said his father beat him with a stick until he bled, then threw down the stick, growling, "I dassen't do this anymore for fear I'll kill you." He said that his mother kept praying out loud and told him over and over again, "God hates you and is gonna send you straight t' hell!"

Jimmy remembers being so frightened and angry that he shouted back, "If God hates me, then I hate Him and I'm glad He died and suffered!"

Because of his age, he was not held responsible for his act. The death was entered officially as an accident and Jimmy was returned to his parents' custody. The psychologist's report, however, suggests that Mr. and Mrs. Wilson were convinced that their son was possessed by the devil and would have preferred to be rid of him. Later investigation revealed the validity of these suspicions.

It was learned that the Wilsons did make several attempts to surrender Jimmy. A neighbor recalled that they had first taken the boy to the town clerk's office but there were told that they were in the wrong place and that they should "calm down and sleep over it." Next they went to a family agency but, when they became frightened by the multitude of questions, they left, saying they had changed their minds.

On the following day, they took the advice of another neighbor and visited the nearby welfare office. They were asked to come back after lunch. When they returned, they were advised to take Jimmy to the children's home in the next town.

Apparently, the delay was too much for the Wilsons to cope with. That evening, Jimmy was found on the steps of a church fifty miles from his home. He was dressed in his best clothes and in a state of shock, numb and mute. Pinned to his shirt was a piece of brown paper torn from a grocery bag, on which was scrawled in pencil: "This here is our James. He be six next month. We dont want him. God dont want him. Nobody want him. Pleez take good kare of him."

The policeman who found him took him to a temporary shelter for homeless children. There he was examined by a doctor, who determined that there was no physical basis for his muteness. Jimmy's photograph was published in the local newspapers in an effort to locate his family or find someone who might know him. It did not take long for several neighbors to come forward and identify the child.

They led the way to the ramshackle dwelling that Jimmy called home. It had been cleared of its few worthwhile possessions. Clearly, the Wilsons had piled into their old car and disappeared after abandoning Jimmy.

Now the town clerk, the family agency and the welfare worker who had been unable to assist the Wilsons in properly disposing of their son volunteered to lend active, eager support in the search for Jimmy's parents. But their efforts were of no avail. The Wilsons were never located. Jimmy's history had to be compiled, detective-fashion, from various sources.

The child became a ward of the court and was placed in a religiously sponsored residence for neglected children. In this glorified orphanage, Jimmy's behavior was, by his own admission, "pretty awful," and he confided to a social worker, "I got a spanking almost every day."

Jimmy was given a thorough psychological and neurological examination. His difficulties were diagnosed as "primarily a personality problem" and it was considered imperative that he have a dependable father figure to whom he could relate. Intensive psychotherapy was advised but funds were not available for the purchase of such therapy. The alternative was to foster Jimmy out to a family well-known to the agency supervising his case, but the choice proved unfortunate.

This couple, like Jimmy's own parents, were deeply religious, though more from sincere devotion than fanatical fervor. In addition, Jimmy's foster brother, three years his senior, was exemplary in his behavior. This led to Jimmy being compared unfavorably with this superior boy, whose faultless deportment he could not possibly hope to match. Jimmy made his animosity clear by urinating in his bed, on the living-room carpet and all over his foster brother's Sunday suit. For each such incident, he was clouted soundly by his foster father and ordered to repeat his daily prayers in triplicate by his foster mother.

Jimmy responded adversely to such discipline. He scrawled filthy words across the living-room wall with a heavy black crayon, stuck a twig into the vagina of the family poodle and tore the family Bible into shreds. Thoroughly disgusted, his foster parents returned him to the agency with the admission that they had accepted the boy more out of religious "duty" than out of any true feeling for the child himself.

It was at this point that the agency, convinced that Jimmy could not yet contend with a foster home but equally convinced that he was sure to deteriorate quickly in a closed institutional setting, contacted Montanari. The agency could only afford to pay eighty dollars a month toward Jimmy's tuition but asked Monty to accept the boy as a favor to them.

"Not as a favor to you," wrote back Montanari, "but as a favor to Jimmy. I know that you people don't really think too much of us because we don't have a professional staff. But we're different in other ways, too. Unlike the traditional approach of raising the money before you accept the child, we do the reverse. So send the boy to me. Let me talk to him. If I think we can help him, I'll accept him and we'll worry about getting the money later."

Recalling his first meeting with Jimmy, Montanari says, "I

felt very sorry for this boy when I heard about all he'd been through, but I had mixed feelings about taking him. Then, after I met him and had a chance to talk to him, I forgot everything I knew about him. Jimmy impressed me as just a scared little rabbit. We seemed to relate to each other. I felt something for this boy, what the psychiatrists call empathy. Maybe Jimmy and me, we needed each other for some reason; maybe that's why we got along so well, I don't know. Anyway, I knew for sure I was going to do what I could for this kid. But I didn't tell my staff anything about his background. I didn't want to take any chances on influencing their attitude to the boy. I let them play it by ear. Take him the way he *is*, don't worry about the way he *was*—that's part of my concept of teaching kids like Jimmy."

Immediately after accepting the boy, Monty took him to the Dade County Child Guidance Clinic for evaluation. Dr. Richard Emerson, the Clinic's youthful director, comments: "It seems pretty clear that Jimmy was the sort of child who would have no place to go if Monty hadn't accepted him, for there just aren't resources available for such children. Jimmy was diagnosed here as showing evidence of harboring great guilt and exhibiting a tremendous need for self-punishment. Perhaps even more important, he was found to be a very sad child with a desperate need to be needed, but with no basic relationships around which to orient his sense of values and his view of the world. It was Monty's job to give him these things."

At first, Jimmy attempted to shut out everyone: teachers, house parents, classmates. He plugged his ears with clay so that he wouldn't have to listen. Monty recalls that the youngster ate soap, paste and toilet paper to inflict punishment upon himself and remarks, "This child was obsessed with the feeling that somebody was after him. He used to scream 'God is punishing me!' and would climb all the way up to the top of the highest tree, or dig a tunnel under one of the sand piles in the backyard and crawl down into it. He was trying to disappear because he couldn't believe that anybody gave a damn about him. He kept testing our love and would say to me or one of my staff, 'Are you my friend even though I'm bad? Would you still love me if I killed someone? Could you breathe in a whole bunch of gas and still be my friend?' I've never seen a boy so guilty and frightened."

Alver Louys recalls how Jimmy's unpredictable behavior led her to keep a switch—a tree twig—on the windowsill of her classroom. "When Jimmy became restless and got up to walk out, I'd take a swipe at his legs and that would make him stay in his seat," she says. "But one day Monty walked in and spotted that switch. He didn't say a word, just took it off the windowsill, snapped it in two and tossed it into the wastebasket. But I got the message and never used a switch again."

The incident did not escape Jimmy's notice and served to strengthen the boy's relationship with Monty. "It gave me an edge with him," Montanari agrees, "even though I didn't plan it that way. But Jimmy's defenses were up pretty high. He was very reluctant to trust anybody, including me. I tried taking him to basketball games. I took him home with me for dinner and let him stay overnight. I wanted to win his confidence, you see."

Monty's wife, Carol—known to the youngsters as "Aunt Carol" or "Mrs. Monty"—adds, "Jimmy behaved like a little angel when he visited us but you could sense his resistance. He didn't really have faith in anyone. You could see that he wanted to open up but something kept holding him back. He just couldn't do it."

Jimmy's inner confusion was apparent when, for example, he would ask to be excused from class to draw pictures by himself in a corner. When granted permission to pursue the activity he wished, he would invariably find himself unable to do anything at all and would scream, "See, that's what I mean, I don't want to do anything but you want me to!"

On the one hand, he resented the few limits placed on him. On the other, he pleaded for limits, for this indicated that someone cared and gave him a sense of belonging. His logic was topsy-turvy. In the manner of the emotionally disturbed, he did things that were unreasonable to others but perfectly reasonable to himself.

He was, for example, a perfectionist. His one-track mind would not tolerate mistakes. If he made an error in class, he would tear up his paper at once. "I saw him do this time after time," Montanari recalls. "One day, I took him aside and said to him, 'Jimmy, why do you think they put erasers on pencils? Do you know why?' Well, he just looked at me, didn't answer, and so I answered my own question. 'To correct mistakes, that's why,' I told him. I tried to make him understand that everybody makes mistakes, that nobody's perfect, and that's why the eraser was invented. I showed him how to use the eraser and got him interested in rubbing it over the paper himself. I showed him how it could save him doing all his work over again and tried to make erasing seem like fun. Well, it took a long while, but he eventually got around to using an eraser instead of tearing up his schoolwork. I think, in a way, that this was Jimmy's first real step in overcoming his fears."

After many months of devoted effort on the part of Monty and his staff, Jimmy's fears began to dwindle. He started to make friends and took a particular liking to "Paul the Potato," who was younger and from whom he seemed to gain a sense of importance. As his defenses diminished, his abilities in the classroom increased. When complimented on his imaginative play at the sandpile, he would respond happily, "Wasn't it a good idea I brought my good ideas along today?"

He began to savor the compliments that were handed out judiciously by Monty and his staff. In fact, he became so eager for compliments that he would spend much of his spare time working with hammer and nails to devise some small gift for Monty, a teacher or a house parent, and present it, saying, "I made this for you because I want you to like me better than any of the other boys."

This emotional blackmail was not encouraged by Montanari. "I made it clear to my staff," he says, "that they should accept such gifts graciously but be careful not to let themselves be bought by this boy. Jimmy had to understand that he was loved just for being himself, not for the presents he made. More important, we had to get across the fact that we loved him even when we didn't understand him. The love, you see, has to come first if you want to help children like Jimmy. So we overlooked his aggressiveness, his vulgarity and his pettiness. We disregarded his past. Then we saw that here was a lovely child, after all, who simply had never gotten an even break in life."

As Jimmy's social behavior improved, he began to take pride in uncovering mischief-making among his peers and reported his observations to Monty or a member of the staff. On several such occasions, visitors were present and expressed disdain at what they termed "ratting."

"I get mad as hell when people talk that way," Montanari says. "I mean, this is the boy's way of showing that he is finally learning to respect law and order. When a normal kid reports on his classmates in public school, he's called a monitor. And when a grown man goes to the authorities to expose a law-breaker, he's called a good citizen. But when a sick little boy does it in order to grow up and find some self-respect, he's criti-cized and condemned. Why? Because he's emotionally disturbed, that's why. Some people just can't ever forget it."

When funds for Jimmy's care and education ran far below the cost of maintenance, Montanari forsook pride for necessity and devoted his out-of-school hours to coaxing dollars from the more affluent members of the community. At one time, he wrote to the agency that had referred Jimmy: "I've raised a little scholarship money for the boy from a local builder who is a friend of the school. I put the bite on him to donate material to fix up one of my cottages and, in return, I took what it would have cost me—about $250—and gave it to Jimmy as a scholar-ship in the name of the company."

When his resourcefulness failed to produce further funds, he went to his favorite benefactors, the Opti-Mrs. Club, and pleaded, "I have taught this boy. Each day I see improvement. When he first came to me, his IQ was only 60. Now it is 115. I call that progress. But I've run out of money. I need your help to go on."

As always, the Opti-Mrs. Club came through, this time for Jimmy. They arranged a fund-raising luncheon in his behalf at which the guest of honor was another Jimmy—Jimmy Piersall, the famous baseball player, who, by his own admission, had suf-fered an emotionally disturbed childhood. Jimmy Piersall had written a book about his life which was transformed into a motion picture titled *Fear Strikes Out.* When he visited the Montanari Clinical School, he played catch with Jimmy Wilson and the other children. "Emotional disturbance can happen to anybody," he told the visitors who dropped by to see him. "I know. It happened to me."

More than any other child in the school, Jimmy Wilson was deeply affected by the big-league ballplayer's visit. He began to badger Montanari, "Hey, come on Monty, let's play ball. How about it?"

This pleased Montanari greatly, for here was a healthy outlet for Jimmy's emotions. From that moment on, he took time out each afternoon to play catch with the little towhead who was at last beginning to shake off his guilt, his hostility and his deeply imbedded fears. The hour or so of play likewise afforded him opportunity to size up the boy's emotional progress unobtrusively, and he concluded that Jimmy was ready to be discharged if a good foster family could be found for him.

Before many weeks had gone by, Montanari came upon a couple in their late thirties who were childless. For more than ten years they had tried, without success, to adopt a child. At first they had been refused because they were "too young and should keep trying to have one of your own" and, in later years, they were told that they were "too old to take on such an important responsibility." In the years between, they had been refused for reasons ranging from "inadequate income"—he was the captain of a fishing boat, earning a moderate salary—to "educational insufficiency"—neither had completed high school.

Montanari scorns such attitudes and says angrily, "It's a damned shame that good people like these were denied a child all those years. Nobody stops mama from having a child of her own no matter how old she is or how little money she's got. Nobody dares to accuse her of being an inadequate parent. But there's so much red tape with most adoption agencies that it seems like people are only considered inadequate as parents when they beg to love and care for some poor little orphan. I've seen a hell of a lot of kids shoved aside because some agency was just too fussy about picking homes for these kids. So what happens to them? They rot away in institutions somewhere."

Convinced that he had found a good family for Jimmy, Montanari contacted Mrs. Louise Alpert, general casework supervisor of the Children's Service Bureau of Dade County, who would have to approve his choice. "This couple is so anxious for a child that they'd take a horse if it had two legs," he told her enthusiastically. "They're wonderful people. The husband is a hard-working guy who seems to be very much in love with his wife. She's a plain gal, a really good person, and she told me that she herself was an adopted child, so she has a pretty good understanding of what Jimmy's up against. As for the boy, he seems to be crazy about his prospective mama and daddy."

Mrs. Alpert admits that she was impressed but more cautious. "Jimmy needs a great deal of love and attention," she remembers telling Monty. "It would certainly be best for him to be placed with a family like this where there are no other children. But does this couple impress you as the sort who can administer the kind of steady discipline that Jimmy needs? Can they set limits the way you do at the school, with the same sort of kindness and understanding?"

Montanari assured her that the prospective foster parents were as ideal as one could hope for and that a youngster with Jimmy's background was most fortunate to have such a couple eager to take him into their home. After obtaining approval of the Children's Bureau, he had to secure approval of the Florida State Welfare Department and the agency that had sent Jimmy to him in the first place. Following several conferences with Monty, Jimmy and his prospective parents, approval became unanimous.

In his last day at the Clinical School, Jimmy wrote a short composition in class on the subject "My Hero." He wrote, "My hero is not discovered yet. But my new parents could be heroes for saving me from going to more foster homes."

Two weeks later, Monty received a letter from Jimmy's foster mother. "My husband and Jimmy," she wrote, "play softball in the backyard every afternoon and Jimmy helps me in the garden. All of us are having wonderful times together. But the most wonderful day of my life was the day that Jimmy looked up at me after dinner and then gave me a big kiss. 'You're the best cook in the whole wide world, Mommy,' he said to me. It was the first time he ever called me Mommy. Oh, it felt good!"

Six months later, Jimmy was legally adopted, despite his age —he was eight, an "unadoptable" age generally—and despite his background.

"Jimmy was a lucky boy," comments Montanari, "but no luckier than the couple who took him into their home as their son. Because they needed him, you see, as much as he needed them. I always feel particularly grateful to people like that because when I discharge a child, he has to have a loving home to go to, he has to have parents who can pick up where we leave off."

Appended to the files of "Paul the Potato" and Jimmy, "the five-year-old killer," is this brief comment by an elated Montanari: "These are two kids we go to Heaven for!"

Stimulated by such successes and pressed to accommodate more children, he added a new wing to his facilities. The new wing was dedicated at an open-house ceremony on February 1, 1959, and a local columnist reported that "the air was filled with praises for the splendid work being done."

Three weeks later, however, Montanari received notice from the city attorney that the Hialeah City Council, by unanimous motion, held that his major school and residence located in Deer Park, an upper-middle-class neighborhood, was being operated in violation of local zoning ordinances. He was given sixty days, in effect, to either shut down or get out.

Astonished by the sudden change in attitude, Montanari protested to inquiring newsmen, "Whatever success I've had, I owe to the goodwill of this community. My kids need good neighbors. Sure, I had to use more of my grounds because my school was growing. But before I added a new classroom or another bathroom, I talked it over with my neighbors. They told me to go right ahead and gave me their blessing. So did the city. They renewed my license every year. Nobody ever made a formal complaint to me. Now suddenly thirty-six residents of Deer Park form a homeowners' association, hire a lawyer, go behind my back and file a petition with the City Council, and the City Council says I have to move. Where? To the swamps? Well, damn it, I can't raise kids with the alligators!"

On February 28, for refusing to comply with the order, Montanari was arrested for adversely affecting the "peace and dignity" of the neighborhood, and was booked, mugged and jailed.

VIII

IT WAS CHARACTERISTIC OF Montanari to respond in this fashion
to what he considered "intimidation and harassment." As a
child, he had been raised to respect social justice above all else.
As a youth, he had tested "the establishment" and found it over-
whelmed by "red tape and double-talk." As a young adult, he
had become an iconoclast, impatiently brushing aside "the false
gods of pretense, protocol and pedantry." Now he was a full-
blown maverick who could not countenance either the legal
barriers or the social lethargy which stood in the way of attending to the needs of emotionally disturbed children.

His bitterness in recounting his experience in 1959 is un-
mistakable, but it is a bitterness tinged more with sorrow and
disillusionment than with anger or despair. "Those people who
signed the petition said they had nothing against me personally,"
he recollects. "Neither did the City Council. They liked me fine,
they said, but they just didn't want me in Deer Park. One of
their complaints was that I kept two cars in my driveway and
they claimed that this constituted a safety hazard. Well, lots of
my neighbors had two cars but I didn't complain. I needed those
cars to transport my kids to the recreational facilities in the area.
You see, it wasn't *me* they didn't want. It was *my kids*. They
called them 'those crazy little kids down the street.' Well, the
way I look at things, my kids are human beings the same as
theirs and I have more people looking after mine than they do.

If I'd let them put me out of business, my kids would have no place to go and I couldn't let that happen. I had to fight back." In fighting back, Monty became a minor cause célèbre. Other neighbors in Deer Park as well as civic leaders, professional people, members of the clergy and the press rallied to his support. Larry Thompson, popular columnist of the *Miami Herald*, summed it up in these words:

Strong as my feelings are for the school, it can't be denied that the neighbors have their rights. But the children in the Montanari school know nothing of legal rights and privileges. They are not even conscious of the fact that they have a right to learn how to adjust themselves and that it is a privilege for them to be receiving this training in such a school. It will be a shame—a tragic shame—if arrangements are not made for the Montanari Clinical School to continue to help children who, through no fault of their own, cannot help themselves. It is needed—not only by the children but by the community, if the community has a conscience.

To this quiet appeal for compassionate understanding, one member of the Deer Park Homeowners' Association replied, "We have our problems, too; we have a neighborhood we are proud of." Their attorney asserted that "the homeowners cannot compromise a city ordinance." And the Hialeah City Council said, "We are not the enforcing body, we just make the laws and it is up to the enforcing agency to see that they are carried out."

Here, in microcosm, the dynamics of contemporary social discrimination were being enacted. Here was being demonstrated the inadequacy of laws which all too often fail to reflect true social justice.

A local psychiatrist expressed this discrepancy in blunter language when he remarked, "These people who invoke the zoning law supposedly to preserve the peace and dignity of their neighborhood simply don't want handicapped children around. They use zoning to cover up their real feelings."

Dr. E. Paul Benoit, then chief psychologist of the Governor Bacon Health Center in Delaware, made clear his distress at the possibility that the school might be shut down:

Somehow, I am not satisfied with the reason that the rights of neighbors are being violated. I spent three days at the school last fall while it was in full operation. Noise level was within bounds. Traffic was not affected significantly. A dignified professional project is being conducted. *The school is unquestionably a very great community asset.* It returns improved children to their families at an exceedingly high rate. But the socializing of difficult children cannot be done in the abstract. The locale is also important. There must be repeated contact with community life so that the children can try their hand at independent activity and the director can test their capacity and readiness to assume their place in society. From this standpoint, the school is in an ideal location. Removal to an isolated spot would diminish its efficiency.

The manager of the neighborhood Essex Theater volunteered an interesting observation on the attendance of Monty's children at the movie house. "Mr. Montanari doesn't let them see just any movie," he said. "He carefully selects their entertainment. They act beautifully in here, obedient to their teacher and polite to everyone. They never cause any trouble whatsoever, which is more than I can say for some of the so-called normal children."

Discussing the matter in retrospect, Hialeah's leading citizen, Mayor Henry Milander, admitted candidly, "Some of Monty's emotionally disturbed children are better behaved than the normal kids here. They might bust a window but so what? Other kids do it every day. We get complaints every day."

But the mayor did not testify at Monty's trial, which took place on Friday, the thirteenth of May, 1959, in a hot, stuffy courtroom crowded with interested spectators.

Herbert P. Benn, attorney for the Deer Park Homeowners' Association, pleaded that the court consider only the legal, and not the emotional, aspects of the case. "I will concur that Mr. Montanari has been doing a fine job," he assented, "but that is not the issue at stake."

Monty's attorney, Abe Aronovitz, countered:

It is inconceivable to me that neither the mayor of this city, the zoning and building officials, nor the police department had not passed, seen, observed or heard this school and not complained about it until now. The cruelest thing that can happen in a governmental way is when some neighbors bring pressure. Children are children, and if a person is offended by a child, he may be offended by the whistling of a bird or the falling of a leaf. There has been no statement that this is a bad school. How can you be asked to remove a school not because it is improperly run but because it is improperly located? That is wrong. This man is doing God's work.

Harsh words were exchanged on both sides with the result that the legal arguments were generating more heat than light. Finally, Judge Frank Imand pounded his gavel to clear the air.

"Let's not kid ourselves, gentlemen," he said, controlling his exasperation with difficulty. "I believe the whole issue before us is simply that certain residents in that area are getting sick and tired of having Montanari operate a school for disturbed children."

Refusing to countenance any objections, he stated angrily that "pressure" had been put upon him day and night since the trial began. "My telephone has been ringing," he informed the courtroom. "I was told to do this, do that. Well, I'm going to rule in the case according to the law and they can like it or not. If they want to fire me tomorrow, they can fire me."

He ruled that the law made clear that local zoning regulations could not discriminate between public and private schools, that the Clinical School served public as well as private interest, and that Montanari could not therefore rightfully be judged guilty of violating the zoning code. Then, with a rap of his gavel, he acquitted Monty of the charges brought against him.

Upon hearing the decision, Monty wept openly, unashamedly. Spectators were simultaneously startled and deeply moved by the incongruous sight of this stocky, virile-looking man giving way to such a display of emotion. Tears continued to stream down his cheeks as he mumbled to reporters, "It's a victory for my children."

On the following day, the *Miami Herald* printed a letter from a woman who had witnessed the trial and who commented:

The judge's decision based on the law that a private school enjoys the same privileges of location as a public school also included the premise that the advantage of the many overrules the inconvenience to the few. So justice admits that the children of the Montanari school, while unacceptable to tax-supported schools, are children with the right to self-development in a neighborhood which contributes beauty to their environment. Judge Imand ruled according to the civil laws involved, but we felt that there also emanated from the bench the Law of Love.

In gratitude, Montanari has willed his school to the city of Hialeah. He has added new facilities, but not in Deer Park. That house—his family's first home, where he established the Clinical School—serves as school and residence for the older boys. His newer facilities are no more than a block or two away, in equally respectable residential sections. He obtained them as demands for his services increased, as favorable opportunities arose to make such acquisitions practical and as his credit standing appreciated to the point where he could capitalize on opportunities for expansion.

Montanari's own personal credit was supported by the private contributions of affluent local businessmen such as Lee Ratner, a well-known real-estate executive, whose generous donation helped Monty to refurbish the Deer Park facility and in whose honor the name Ratner House was bestowed on that school and residence.

The Opti-Mrs. Club arranged many fund-raising affairs for the school's benefit. Most people do not realize that the prominent celebrities who contribute their services to such causes frequently receive a most generous fee for their appearances. When, for example, a well-known entertainer appeared at a leading Miami Beach hotel in Monty's behalf, tickets sold for twenty-five dollars in order to cover the entertainer's substantial fee and the cost of the facilities as well as a small profit for the school. Buddy Hackett, on the other hand, donated his entire fee to the school and made possible the erection of a playhouse for the children which has, in appreciation, been named the Buddy Hackett Auditorium.

Despite the private nature of the enterprise, examination of Montanari's books reveals that, even today, no sophisticated investor would consider the Clinical School a moneymaking venture. A great number of parents default on payments for tuition and treatment of their children; some forty beds are kept in reserve for indigent youngsters residing in the area; no child, from any state or any part of the world, is turned away for inability to pay.

"If I wanted to get rich," says Monty with a careless shrug of his shoulders, "I wouldn't have chosen this kind of work in the first place."

Residential care still remains at three hundred dollars a month for children under twelve, four hundred dollars for older children who require extra care. Welfare remunerations rarely meet the cost of maintaining their referrals. This fact prompted Dr. Povl W. Tousseing—formerly with the Menninger Foundation, now chief of the Child Psychiatric Department at Oklahoma City Medical School—to warn Monty:

The need in this nation for low-cost treatment is so enormous that you can find yourself stuck with the welfare loads of the entire United States if you don't watch out. By accepting children on the national level at below cost, you will merely be perpetuating the hopelessly inadequate welfare payments made for the care of children everywhere. Your full fee is not unreasonable for many welfare departments across the states and, at the same time, by having sufficient full fee paying students, you will be able to carry out some of the plans which otherwise will have to wait indefinitely. This is in no way cruelty, and actually will place you on a solid footing to eventually offer much more for every treatment dollar.

Montanari's answer was to expand his professional staff at the expense of his personal income as more referrals came his way. Dr. Leo Grossman, a well-known Miami pediatrician who is the school's medical director, shakes his head in bewilderment and says of Monty, "This man is a nut! In the ten years I've known him, he's blown half his dough on kids who can't afford his services. That's why he's broke all the time. He's sentimental. He takes hopeless kids and sometimes works miracles with them. He's all heart. He won't let anything stand in his way as far as helping these youngsters is concerned. He devotes his entire life to this thing."

Dr. Grossman has put his finger on a fundamental difference between Monty and most of his colleagues: his intensely personal involvement with the children in his care. They are as much a part of his private life as is his own family, and he is fortunate in that his family recognizes this.

His children work at the school during their summer vacations, helping out in the office, assisting the teachers and playing with the youngsters. Monty has expressed his pride in Gary and Cissy by naming one cottage Gary House, after his son; another Adele House, after his daughter's given name; and a third Karen House, for his stepdaughter.

His wife, Carol, is equally devoted to the school. It is apparent to those who know the Montanaris that Carol's empathy with Monty—his goals, his idiosyncrasies, his sensitivity—parallels remarkably Monty's empathy with the children entrusted to his care. She has drawn generously from her personal income to enable Monty to extend his help to more indigent youngsters.

The Montanari home is in North Miami, only minutes away from the Clinical School. Their ranch-style home is modest, tastefully furnished but unpretentious. Telephones are numerous throughout the house and are apt to ring at any moment of the day or night.

Monty takes no days off. He works seven days a week and is on call twenty-four hours a day, every day. "When you're dealing with emotionally disturbed kids," he says, "you have to expect an emergency at any time."

A case in point is Alice Kohler, an awkward, gawky, fidgety thirteen-year-old, referred by an out-of-state family agency that described her as "severely disturbed, a petty thief and prone to suicide." Alice had been tabbed "the orphan with parents" by those who knew her, because Mr. and Mrs. Kohler were so unaware of their daughter's emotional difficulty.

"On the surface," explains Monty, "the Kohlers were pretty decent people. They were pleasant, had lots of friends and nobody could say a bad word about them. They didn't drink, didn't screw around, didn't do a damn thing that was wrong.

But they were false parents because they never gave Alice anything resembling love, respect or attention. The child was emotionally abandoned in her own home. She was born by accident, you see, but they refused to face up to it. They didn't dislike her but they didn't like her either. When Alice became more and more difficult to handle and was finally tossed out of public school, the Kohlers consulted a family agency. The agency referred Alice to me."

In discussing the case, Montanari makes clear his annoyance with parents like the Kohlers. "It's hard to raise hell with people like this," he says. "I mean, they seem so fine, so good, so decent. They don't beat up their kid, they don't let her run wild, they don't even bawl the hell out of her. But they never really stand up for her. They just seem to be going through the motions of being good parents. If I say to them, for example, 'Your child is a holy terror,' they agree with me and try to pacify me. Well, damnit, I don't need pacifying, but I do need some reassurance that mama and daddy have enough love for their child to back her up even while they admit that she is a problem. But their attitude makes me feel that they've really turned against their child and withdrawn their support. It's almost as if they said to me, 'If our child is no good, it's not our fault, so now it's up to you.' Well, this is wrong, all wrong. Parents like this don't want to face up to things. They're good people but they're lousy parents. They just don't really care enough about their kids. They're loveless but not malicious. They fool everybody—their neighbors, their families, themselves —but not their child. And this is the kind of home Alice came from."

Ray Goode, director of the Dade County Welfare Department, who refers many children to Monty, observes, "We find many cases where, on the surface, the home looks basically sound, but when we dig into the thing, we find that it really isn't."

There was little doubt that Alice Kohler came from just such a home. True to form, her parents found numerous reasons to avoid making the trip to Florida. Instead, she was accompanied by a social worker associated with the family agency.

Because the social worker had to catch an early-evening plane back, Monty had one of his staff prepare to drive her to the nearby airport in the school's station wagon. But Alice hated to see her leave. The social worker suggested that it might be a good idea for Alice and her new roommates to go along for the ride, thinking that perhaps it would soften the break between them. "She asked if it was all right with me," Montanari recalls, "and I said, if you think it will make things easier for Alice, fine, take her along to the airport."

Ten minutes after the station wagon returned to the school, Monty's telephone rang. He picked it up and the distraught social worker screamed into his ear, "Mr. Montanari, I've been robbed! My plane is due to leave in less than half an hour and somebody's stolen my ticket and all the money from my handbag!"

He told her not to worry, that he'd be right over. Fifteen minutes later, he arrived at the airport, purchased another ticket and replaced the stolen funds. Monty returned to the school to find Alice's house mother waiting for him in his office.

"Monty, I just found this airplane ticket and forty-two dollars in Alice Kohler's pocket," she said. "The child admitted she had taken them from her social worker's handbag when she wasn't looking to prevent her from leaving. Shall I punish her in any way?"

"Hell, no," Monty answered. "The child's been punished all her life. Don't upset her anymore. Treat her kindly and have her get ready for bed. I'll stop by to say good night to her before I go home."

It was after nine when Montanari returned home. It was almost midnight when he was awakened by the telephone. Again, it was Alice's house mother, but this time her voice was more urgent. "Oh, my God, Monty, you'd better rush over here. Alice has swallowed half a bottle of aspirin. She must have taken it from her social worker's handbag along with the money and hidden it under her mattress. The child is trying to do away with herself."

Commenting on the episode, Montanari says grimly, "This is the kind of call I dread most. The child who gulps down pills, the small boy who tries to strangle himself with a belt, the young girl who slashes her wrists with a piece of broken glass. It seems so inconceivable, a little child attempting suicide. But it does happen, despite all our precautions. Thank God no such attempts have ever succeeded. But this desire to rob oneself of life, this in a child, this is the most fearful thing of all, that anyone so young should be so desperate."

Immediately after speaking to Alice's house mother, Monty telephoned Dr. Leo Grossman to come to the school at once. Stopping merely to pull on a pair of slacks and a shirt over his pajamas, Monty arrived at the school in time to assist Dr. Grossman and a nurse, who were pumping out the contents of Alice Kohler's stomach. He remained at her bedside for several hours afterward, until the child was breathing quietly again.

"He just sat there beside her," recalls Alice's house mother, "mopping her forehead with his handkerchief, holding her hand to reassure her that somebody cared, acting as an interested parent might. It was almost dawn by the time he left."

Alice Kohler survived the ordeal that almost claimed her life and remained at the Clinical School for more than a year. "She went back home better able to understand her parents," Montanari explains. "We were successful in helping her to redevelop emotionally, you see, so that her parents—whom I still consider inadequate—could feed her needs. But her needs had diminished to the point where their contribution to Alice's well-being proved to be enough for the child. Her social worker kept tabs on the family for another six months after we discharged her and then she also discharged the family from her care."

For some children, however, there are no such happy endings. Danny Harper was such a child and he presented Montanari with an emergency of a quite different nature.

Danny was a pint-size twelve-year-old who, despite his age and size, could drive an automobile as well as any man. His special passion was Cadillacs, which he loved to appropriate for joy rides. Because of his small stature, he could barely be seen behind the wheel of a car and, for this reason, achieved questionable notoriety as "the invisible driver." Within six months of his enrollment at the Clinical School, Danny had run afoul of the law twice for stealing Cadillacs. Both times, Monty bailed him out. The third occasion involved a distinct intrusion on his private life.

For a week prior to this occurrence, Monty's wife and several friends had been out raising funds for the leukemia ward of Variety Children's Hospital in Miami. They had succeeded in accumulating $784.25 in their coin boxes and, in mild celebration, Carol had invited them to her home for the evening.

"Monty didn't arrive home from the school until after ten," Carol recalls. "He'd been up since six that morning and was pretty exhausted when he came in. He greeted our guests, then went to the bedroom saying he was going to freshen up. I knew better and so did everybody else. I knew he would lie down without even bothering to remove his clothes, squint at the little portable television set beside the bed to take his mind off things, and then doze off. It isn't that he means to be rude. It's just that he puts so much into the children that he's usually too tired to socialize. He doesn't enjoy small talk. If he can't talk about kids, he becomes bored, especially when he's tired. And I could see that this time he was very tired."

He did exactly as Carol expected, except that he didn't have a chance to go to sleep. Just as he was about to nod, lulled by the low voice of a local newscaster on the television set, Monty heard a reference to "a driverless pink Cadillac heading toward the Airport Expressway not far from the Hialeah racetrack."

"As soon as I heard the news break," says Montanari, "I suspected that Danny Harper was behind the wheel of that 'driverless pink Cadillac.' And when I picked up the phone that started to ring, it was Danny's house father. He said he'd just heard the announcement on the radio and was worried because Danny had been given the privilege of attending a basketball game in the local auditorium that evening, so he wasn't in his cottage. He wondered if Danny had gone joy-riding instead. I happened to remember that one of my neighbors had just purchased a pink Cadillac. He kept it in his driveway and I knew that he sometimes forgot to remove the key from the ignition. It made sense to assume that Danny had spotted the car on his way to the basketball game and couldn't resist the impulse to take it for a drive. Chances are he found the key ready and waiting. I told Danny's house father not to notify the police because the boy couldn't afford more trouble with the law, and that I was going after him myself."

Judging from past experience, Montanari reasoned that Danny would be heading toward his grandparents' home in Fort Lauderdale. He seemed to relish terrorizing this elderly couple by barging in and assuming command of their home.

When the roads are clear, as they are in the late evening, the Montanari residence is about twenty minutes' driving time from the point where Golden Glades Drive leads into the intricate cloverleaf of roads that branch off Interstate Highway 95. From this point, both the Sunshine State Parkway and U.S. 441 run north toward Fort Lauderdale.

"I wasn't sure which route Danny might take," explains Montanari in detailing the incident, "so I just pulled up at the turnoff and waited for him to come by. A pink Caddy wouldn't be hard to spot. If my hunch was correct, I'd arrived just in time to intercept the car. So I just sat there waiting and praying. I kept the motor running and my foot on the gas, ready to take off the second I saw Danny go by. It was a pretty tense business because, if I'd misjudged, then I'd have to get the police to help me locate the boy. He was on probation and chances are that if the police became involved, Danny would be sent to reform school. I didn't want this to happen so I sweat it out."

Monty's hunch proved accurate. Within a few minutes, a sleek pink Cadillac loomed up out of the darkness and continued north on U.S. 441. Monty took after the car like a bullet, picking up enough speed to enable him to pull alongside the Cadillac. "Sure enough, it was Danny there behind the wheel," he says. "I could hardly see him, he was down so low in the seat, but I knew it was Danny. He had that steering wheel gripped tight in his hands and his little head was poked back so he could see over the big windshield. Oh, God, he was a nervy little peanut. He was doing about fifty and I didn't dare distract him until he slowed down. So I just slipped in behind him, tailing him, and waited for him to reach a stoplight at one of the intersections a couple of miles ahead."

The moment Danny slowed down for a light, Monty swung his own car alongside, tooted his horn insistently and shouted through the open window, "It's me, Monty! Pull over, Danny, stop the car!" The stunned youngster jammed his foot down on the brake instinctively. Monty swerved sharply in front of him, forcing Danny to bring the Cadillac to a full, screaming stop.

"I jumped out of my car," says Montanari, "and ran back to Danny, shoving my hand through the open window to grab the ignition key. Then I opened the door, took that surprised little boy by the hand and led him over to my car, shoving him in alongside me. Other drivers were honking and cursing at me for blocking their way. I drove off the main highway as quickly as I could, took the key away and ordered Danny not to dare move until I got back. I knew he was too scared to run but I had to make sure. Then I went back to the Caddy and drove it off the highway behind my car. By the time I got back to Danny, I was sweating like a bull."

But by this time, Danny had recovered from his initial shock. He had opened the glove compartment and found a screwdriver. Before Montanari could turn on the ignition, Danny's arm was raised high, with the screwdriver gripped in his right hand like a dagger. His eyes were narrowed to thin slits and his lips were pressed tightly together.

"I sat back in my seat, trying to play it cool and easy," recounts Montanari. "I just looked him straight in the face and said quietly, 'Give me that screwdriver, Danny.' He didn't say a word, just kept pointing the damn thing at me but not making a move to use it. I wasn't sure whether he would or wouldn't but I wasn't taking any chances. As soon as I saw him hesitate, I reached up and knocked the screwdriver out of his hand. All of a sudden the toughness went out of him and he began to hug me, begging me, 'Don't send me to Youth Hall, Monty, please don't send me away, I don't want to go to jail.' And I don't know exactly what I said, I was so upset myself, but it was probably something like 'Goddamnit, you know I'm not going to send you to jail. If I wanted to do that, I'd have let the police come out after you, wouldn't I?' After that, he just cuddled up next to me, said he was sorry for stealing the Caddy and would go back with me to return it if I wanted him to. 'Sure, Danny,' I told him, 'that's what we'll do first thing in the morning.' Then, while I started the car, he put his head on my shoulder and said, 'I'm awful tired out from acting mean, Monty; all I want to do is go to sleep.' And that's just what that little peanut did."

Montanari left the Cadillac parked on the side of the road for the night and drove Danny, not to the school, but to his home. "I thought it would be better for him to stay at my house that night," he explains. "I carried him inside without his ever waking up and Carol peeled off his clothes and put him to bed in the guest room. Early the next morning, Danny and I went and picked up the Caddy, and brought it back to the man who owned it. Danny apologized to him and, luckily, he was a very understanding person. He didn't press charges against the boy."

Why did Danny Harper steal Cadillacs?

"Only God knows," says Montanari with a shrug. "Everyone has a different explanation. A welfare worker said it was because Danny was a deprived child who yearned for the good things in life, and the Cadillac is a status symbol. A psychologist said that it was clear to him that the boy swiped big expensive automobiles to express his resentment of authority, the car's owner, who represented Danny's daddy, whom the boy hates. A court psychiatrist had another notion and blamed it on Danny's shortness. He said the boy had a strong need for masculine identification because he didn't feel like much of a man and that the big car was a phallic symbol. Then the cop who'd picked up Danny once before came up with still another point of view. He decided that Danny was just a little squirt, a wise guy who wanted to be a big shot and that's why he stole Cadillacs. So who is right? Maybe all of them, maybe none of them. This boy had been through so much that everybody was guessing."

Danny Harper was one of those "minor tragedies" that escape the public view. Of illegitimate birth, he was adopted in his second year. His adoptive mother, however, was a sickly, emo-

tionally unstable woman who was committed to a mental institution soon after Danny entered public school. His adoptive
father was a garage mechanic of doubtful character, who was in
frequent trouble with the law. His only pride in Danny rested
on the boy's ability to drive a car before the youngster had
reached his tenth birthday. Not long after the boy had so
proved himself, the father was imprisoned for burglary.

Danny was placed with his paternal grandparents, and his
grandmother, the only source of love in the child's life, admitted, "No one ever really wanted this boy."

Danny's personality soon began to disintegrate. He lied,
cheated and stole, not for reasons of material gain but for
deeper, more personal reasons. He was expelled from school for
truancy, tendencies toward homosexuality and minor acts of
vandalism. After Danny had been at the Dade County Children's
Home in Kendall, Florida, for a short time, a clinical psychologist reported: "It is very clear that an institution such as this
is completely unsuited to this boy's needs and that his condition
has worsened during his stay here. His emotional disturbance is
of severe proportions, marked by a lack of adequate inner control which results in impulsive actions."

At the age of twelve, Danny was made a ward of the Dade
County Juvenile Court and entrusted to the charge of Probation
Officer Carl A. Baughman, who knew Montanari and whose
daughter taught at the Clinical School. At Mr. Baughman's urg-
ing, Monty accepted Danny and the county paid $144 a month
toward his tuition and residential care.

Monty worked with him intensively but the moment he
turned his back, Danny ran amok. He cornered an attractive
young teacher and pinched her breasts "to see if milk would
come." He stole a ride in a farmer's pickup truck loaded with
manure and buried himself under the soft manure because "this
proves I'm nothing but shit." He dressed himself up in girl's
clothing, and lifted the skirt to expose himself, shouting, "Oh,
Jesus Christ, cut them off, I don't want to be a boy anymore!"

One of Danny's house fathers entered this remark on his
record:

He's a terribly mixed-up kid, yet I find myself liking him very much. The fact that he's been diagnosed as a child whose personality has little chance of being changed in society's favor doesn't enter into my opinion of him. I like Danny for something other than pity or sorrow. There is something in this boy that sets him apart but I cannot put my finger on just what it is. I know that he is terribly sick, that the staff is up in arms about him. And I hereby give notice that I no longer want to serve as his house father, not because I cannot stand him, but because I have not yet become immune enough to the despair in this field of work and cannot bear to accept the fact that Danny Harper is beyond help.

The time arrived when Montanari himself could no longer protect Danny. "It was too late to salvage the boy," he says sadly. "After the incident with the Cadillac, Danny regressed again. He became so impossible to manage that my entire staff threatened to quit unless I let him go. There was no alternative. I couldn't help him. He'd passed the point of no return."

He contacted the state child welfare supervisor, who was familiar with Danny's case. The desperate supervisor wrote a moving plea to the authorities: "An evaluation of several years ago denied the existence of psychosis, which negated admittance to the State Hospital, but since long-term institutional care seems indicated, we would like to request a current psychiatric evaluation to determine if the State Hospital might someday be a possibility."

The ironic hope that the child had finally become sick enough to warrant commitment as a mental case proved futile. Danny did not meet the necessary requirements. The diagnosis was: "Adjustment reaction of adolescence with conduct disorder." Montanari's final note to the juvenile authorities reads: "It is with regret that I say that this boy needs the closed institutional setting that we are not able to provide for him. I hope, in lieu of anything else, that the Okeechobee School for Boys will be recommended."

In postscript to the case of Danny Harper, it should be noted that the boy had amassed twelve arrests for misconduct and been on probation four times prior to being remanded to the Okeechobee reformatory. There, his condition continued to deteriorate. Before a year had elapsed, Danny had escaped, stolen a car and, to avoid arrest, fled to the refuge of a small country church. Compelled to "tear something up," he found several rolls of toilet paper in the empty church, ripped them apart and tossed them everywhere. Then he discovered a can of gasoline. For no explainable reason, he drenched the bits of paper with gasoline and put a match to them, fleeing to the woods to watch the conflagration. He was apprehended there shortly after the church had burned to the ground.

The community became enraged and demanded that Danny be sent to the Florida State Prison. Then their indignation went a step further. They demanded that the Okeechobee School for Boys be located elsewhere.

"Because of one boy," says Montanari bitterly, "the community took out their feelings on all the sick kids whose lives are being patched together at Okeechobee. These kids don't live in town. They're already out in the swamps. But they want them buried still farther out."

To Danny Harper, it doesn't matter anymore. At fourteen, he is as good as dead. He has been transferred to a maximum-security cell at the Florida School for Boys in Marianna. He will, in all likelihood, remain here for the rest of his youth and then be moved to a real man-size prison.

His intense emotional confusion shows up starkly in a moving letter he addressed to Montanari upon his installation at Marianna:

DEAR MR. MONTY,

How are you and Mrs. Monty and all my friends? Tell them hello for me. When I get out of here, I would like to work for you. I don't blame the staff for threatening to quit if you kept me in your school. After all, what's a year of a boy's life even if he is a punk, me, when compared to the comfort of a few people like them? There's one thing I've noticed about myself. I do everything right about two-thirds of the way. Like when I went to Kendall for three months, I only stayed two. I kept running till they sent me to the Jackson Hospital and finally kicked me out and sent me to your place. I should have stayed there over a year but was kicked out after eight months. I'm as good as in Apalachicola [state prison] now and don't have to worry anymore. Be sure and thank my friends for coming to court for me and tell the others I don't hold it against them for threatening to quit if you kept me there. I sure would like to live with you like that night when you took me home with you, but I can't. I sure loved that time. I would like to call you dad if it's OK with you. I would like to write the rest of this letter but I can only think of two-thirds of it.

With love, your son,
DANNY.

Montanari watched the boy deteriorate with time, helpless to produce the miracle that would bring him back to society. For it was long ago too late for miracles. The demons that took hold of Danny had such a death grip that neither Monty's best intentions, nor the most intensive psychiatric therapy, nor the latest wonder drugs of modern medicine could shake them loose.

"Failing a child but knowing that someone else can help him is one thing," confides Montanari in a voice husky with emotion. "But failing a child and knowing that there is *no* one else to help him, that you're the end of the line for him, that when you fail, this child is finished—I tell you, this is a terrible thing to live with."

Jack V. Blanton, chief probation officer of the Dade County Juvenile Court, sums up the Danny Harper case with this comment: "It tells a rather morbid and discouraging story of the waste of this little human life. It will be interesting to find out just how much in dollars this boy has already cost the taxpayers."

But the money available is never enough, the early care never sufficient. Dr. Renatus Hartogs, the director of New York City's Youth House, who predicted that Lee Harvey Oswald exhibited dangerous tendencies many years before Oswald assassinated a President of the United States, says, "At least 15 percent of the children I see at Youth House are potential killers. But there is no place for adequate treatment."

And the slain President's brother, New York's Senator Robert F. Kennedy, revealed recently that many children in residence at New York state schools for the mentally deficient are "worse off than animals in a zoo."

The best of care cannot ensure survival for such children, but without the best of care such children have no hope of survival. Public awareness is imperative to prevent these youngsters from becoming the Danny Harpers of tomorrow. For too long, however, a curtain has been drawn to shield polite society from the emotionally disturbed children in their midst.

Sympathy is aroused for the physically damaged child, whose photographs in braces and crutches are used as fund-raising devices. But there is no stigma to physical disability. Emotional disturbance, however, carries its stigma everywhere and institutions that house children with such disabilities lock their doors to visitors.

The Montanari Clinical School is a rare exception. Visitors are welcome there at any time and no apologies are offered if they are shocked by what they see. They are most apt to become shocked at Christmas. For Christmas at Monty's is quite unlike Christmas anywhere else.

IX

THERE ARE NO SNOWBALL FIGHTS, no sleigh rides, no snowmen rising on the lawns. Christmas temperatures hover in the high eighties and the land remains bright with sunshine. Nevertheless, the holiday spirit infects Montanari's children, not simply as a secret wish for a snowfall, or a visit from Santa. Mostly, Christmas is expressed as a longing for home.

You can see it, hear it, feel it, as you tour the grounds. . . .

"I'm gonna see my grandmother and my grandfather for Christmas," says Helen, who is thirteen, "and it's gonna be a wonderful thrill for me. I haven't seen them for almost a year. I'm gonna try to walk from the bus real calm, like a lady. I just hope I'll be able to make it, I'm gonna be so excited. Maybe my mom and dad will be there, too. They're divorced and I haven't seen them since I was a little girl. It sure would be the most wonderful thing that ever happened to me if they would be there. . . ."

Jake, a nine-year-old who walks bent over like a cripple although there is nothing wrong with him physically, and who speaks only in whispers, says huskily, "Santa Claus is my daddy and Mrs. Santa Claus is my mommy. They are coming to get me in a great big car that is magical and will turn into a sled when we reach the North Pole." Jake cannot accept the fact that his parents were killed in an automobile accident. He prefers to live in fantasy. . . .

Angie, with the jet-black hair and eyes to match, is seven. She loves to dance in bare feet. When she isn't dancing, she is singing. But the gaiety is false. "Merry merry Christmas merry merry Christmas merry merry . . ." she chants over and over again, compulsively. Angie still expects to go home for the holiday, unaware that the social worker responsible for her wellbeing has told Montanari, "Her mother will not take her." Montanari asks, "Not even for one day? Can't she put her up Christmas Eve and keep her home just for the holiday?" The social worker shakes her head. "No, Angie's bed is occupied. Her mother has a new boy friend. I have talked to her but it is useless. She is a child herself and she feels threatened by Angie. It is useless. Angie must remain here for Christmas. I will, of course, come to visit her and bring her presents. What else is there to do?" She shrugs her shoulders helplessly. . . .

Snappily dressed in a flashy sport shirt and tailored gabardine slacks, seventeen-year-old Steven sits cross-legged on the grass and squints up at the sky. He says nothing because he has lost temporarily the power of speech. Weeks before Christmas, he had discovered a gift for him hidden in a closet. Inside the box, which he tore open excitedly, was a mammoth kite. He could not wait to fly it. Unable to find a roll of proper string, he used a spool of metallic cord which his parents had purchased to wrap their Christmas gifts. Soon after he got the kite up and flying, an electrical storm erupted and lightning struck the metallic cord. The violent voltage sped down the cord to his hand and smashed into his nervous system so forcibly that he was knocked to the ground. Luckily, he survived the flash but his mind became affected. His frightened, bewildered parents, who lived in the community, brought him to Monty. Dr. Leo Grossman, Monty's medical director, observed that Steven showed symptoms suggesting a reversal of night and day: unusual activity during the evening and total passivity during the daytime. This was symptomatic of serious brain damage and Dr. Howard Engle, specialist in such disorders, was called in as a consultant. He administered neurological tests and an encephalogram—a brain-wave test—and confirmed the diagnosis. He prescribed medical therapy while Monty administered reeducational therapy. The next Christmas, perhaps, would be more meaningful to Steven. . . .

"I sure can't wait to go home," says twelve-year-old Maddy, who is tall, big-boned, physically developed far beyond her years, and has to be restrained from wearing tight blouses and skirts that magnify her buxom figure. "My daddy promised me the greatest Christmas ever," she says proudly. Montanari, however, says frankly, "This is one child I wish I didn't have to send home. When Maddy speaks of her daddy, she means her stepfather. Her real daddy walked out on the family years ago because her mama was whoring around and taking dope. Mama even prostituted Maddy to raise money for dope for herself. Now, this man she's married to . . . well, I can't prove anything, but I have a feeling that every time Maddy goes home for a visit, he goes to bed with her. Mama doesn't give a damn because she's out gallivanting around. Now, I know this is a hell of a thing to say, but I think this is why Maddy is so anxious to go home. She's sexually precocious, you see, and I think she looks forward to making out with her stepfather. She won't tell on him but she's dropped a few hints. So I'm pretty damn sure it's going to be a great Christmas for her new daddy, with Maddy as his Christmas present, but what can I do about it? I can't prove anything. . . ."

Eddie is fourteen, skinny and spindly-legged. He feels worthless. To compensate for this feeling of inadequacy, he has embraced religion. He attends church every Sunday without fail and is a model member of the congregation. During the rest of the week, he is apt to fall to his knees at any time without warning and clasp his hands together in prayer. Eddie's entire family—mother, father and sister—are all undergoing psychoanalysis. Eddie was unable to profit from such therapy. His emotional problems are termed too acute, his personality too unresponsive, and so he had to be isolated from his home. He will return home for Christmas but his family, who despise him for a variety of reasons which are clear only to their individual psychiatrists, do not really want him there. He is sure to receive a cold reception and will probably evidence his disappointment first through prayer, and then through sex. "When Eddie is unhappy," his house father remarks, "he switches from prayer to sex. He has an erection almost constantly." A consulting psychiatrist commented on this phenomenon, "That is just his id popping up." When Montanari heard this, he scoffed. "His id, hell—it's his pecker that keeps popping up!" He adds, by way of explanation, "I get so damned awful tired of these fancy intellectual interpretations. I remember reading once how some psychiatrist analyzed Freud's smoking cigars all the time by saying that the cigar was a symbol of masturbation, and Freud told him, 'Remember, doctor, a cigar is still a cigar!' Well, let's call a cigar a cigar and an erection an erection. Eddie wants to be loved but nobody loves him. Not even at Christmas. . . ."

Stanley is five and runs about in a faded T-shirt and an equally faded pair of denim shorts. He cannot distinguish Christmas from any other time of the year. But his eyes light up when a strange man or woman enters his cottage. "He is looking for his mama and daddy, who never come," says Mrs. Thomasini, his house mother, who is better known to the children as Mama Mia. She is warm and gentle, full of laughter, and she is Italian. She is, in fact, an old friend of Montanari's and, in his early years in Winchendon, Massachusetts, she was frequently his baby-sitter. When she became widowed and had nowhere to turn, he made her a house mother in charge of the youngest children at the school. "I love my babies," she says with a broad smile as she hugs Stanley close to her, "and I spoil 'em all. When they get sick, I get sick with 'em. My children here, they are more good than my own whom I raised. And if I pet them a little bit, it's much better than saying don't do this or don't do that. These little kids, they all want the same thing: kiss 'em and pet 'em and say, 'Little baby, I love you!' Lots of patience and these kids is wonderful. It's just too bad that kids like Stanley, he gotta stay here for Christmas instead of goin' home because at home they got no patience to put up with him there, to change his pants and hug him up a little. Some Christmas for such a wonderful baby!"

For Marian, age ten, overweight and sloppy, Christmas is no different although her parents are far from being disinterested. Both are teachers and very much aware of Marian's emotional instability. "She has no incentive to do her best at school," they wrote to Montanari in a long letter itemizing their daughter's shortcomings. "As she grows older, she shows less and less ability to control her emotions. She jumps from high spirits to tears and tantrums. With all our awareness and sophistication, we cannot help her. Perhaps we are too close to her to help her resolve what we think are deep neurotic conflicts in her personality." Marian keeps going through the motions of joining her classmates' interest in the Christmas holiday but cannot quite comprehend its significance. "You going home, too?" she asks one after the other of her roommates as they make ready to visit their families. And when they leave for home, she weeps, not because she cannot go home but because they have gone and left her. . . .

Harold is fifteen, a long, lanky youth. He is bright, charming and manipulative. He helps to look after the younger boys, for which he is paid by Montanari, but complains loudly to Mary Everett, the attractive principal of the school for the very young, "I got thirty-five dollars from the bank to buy my mother a Christmas present but you won't let me have the money. Why? It's mine. Why can't I have it?" He follows her about the grounds, alternately whining and screaming. Mary Everett allows him to do so without ever raising her voice, because she is a "pro." She understands Harold and she understands Montanari's philosophy. She has worked at the school for two years. She met her husband—John Everett, one of the supervisors— here, and the small house in which they lived for the first few days of their marriage was named Honeymoon Cottage in their honor. She says quietly now, "Harold, I know that you have a check for thirty-five dollars but it is made out to the school. If you will go to one of the stores at the shopping center and select a gift for your mother's Christmas present, I'm sure that Mr. Monty will OK the purchase for you. But the check is not made out to you, it is made out to the school, you must understand that."

Harold complains bitterly and demands to speak to Montanari himself. "I want to buy my mother a nice Christmas present," he pleads, tears welling in his eyes, "and that's

why I want you to please give me my check to do what I want
with." Later, Monty says, "Settle down now, Harold. You know
that the check is not made out to you. But I will back you up
for whatever you want to buy your mama. Just go to the store,
pick out what you want and charge it to me." Harold complains
bitterly, insisting that he is being discriminated against, and
accuses Montanari of withholding his personal funds.

You listen and you become convinced that this boy is being
taken advantage of. Then Monty says to you, "Harold is a great
manipulator. It is part of his sickness. He is only fifteen, but I
have seen him talk a local bank into cashing checks for him.
What he has done now is manipulate another local bank. He
telephoned the bank with which his parents have an account,
talked them into issuing a check for deposit to his account at
the school. But the check was made out to the school, not to
him, and he is doing everything possible to force us to cash the
check for him on the pretense that he needs the money to buy
his mama a Christmas present."

But when Montanari brings such matters to the attention of
Harold's parents, they invariably reply, "Not my Harold! He's a
good boy!" It is their standard response. When Harold was
caught smoking at the age of twelve; when Harold was sum-
moned to the dean's office in eighth grade for drawing carica-
tures of his female classmates in the nude; when Harold brought
to school a weather doll—the skirt treated with cobalt chloride,
which caused it to turn pink when the humidity was high—and
announced that he possessed the only doll that menstruated—
at all such times, his parents threw up their hands in disbelief,
exclaiming, "Not my Harold!" Even after Harold was dismissed
from the public-school system and enrolled at Montanari's, they
persisted in denying every indication of emotional disturbance
in their son. As a result, Harold's ambivalent feelings toward his
parents becomes extreme on special occasions such as birthdays,
anniversaries and Christmas. . . .

In a cottage housing eight boys in their pre-teens, freckle-
faced Oliver lies stretched out, fully clothed, in his bunk. He
lies stiffly, fearful of moving a single muscle, for he has become
convinced that his legs are growing to extraordinary length and

that the least motion on his part will cause his circulation to accelerate and his legs to grow longer and longer. He can go home for Christmas but doesn't dare do so for fear that, in his own home, the process of growth will be speeded up. Miss Dee, his house mother, has twelve grandchildren of her own but seems younger than her years. She has played softball professionally and often plays ball with the youngsters in her charge. Now she approaches Oliver, smacking a baseball against the pocket of the well-oiled fielder's mitt she wears on her left hand, and says, "Come on, Ollie, let's play ball. It will be good for you." But Oliver ignores her, just as he ignores his roommates, who pass by his bunk as they go about decorating the cottage. "Ollie's going to become a giant for Christmas," says one boy. "He told me so himself. He said that after Christmas he'd shrink back to being normal again." On overhearing this remark, Oliver's pale face lights up with the suggestion of a smile. . . .

Across the street is a cottage where reside the most seriously damaged boys of all. They range in age from eight to seventeen. "We haven't a single child here who can actually read a letter and comprehend what's in it," says the house mother. Here are Ralph and Edgar, so helpless that they require the full-time attention of a teacher who is theirs alone. Here is Mort, ten years old and handsome as a Greek god. His speech is a low moan and, in times of high excitement, is full of spit and gurgling as his vocal chords strive valiantly to carry out the orders of his muddled brain. He is preoccupied with measuring things, using a towel twirled tightly into a kind of rope. He lays it against the Christmas tree and calls out, "Foooooorteen . . . feeeeeeefteen . . . seeeeeeexteen . . ." Watching him closely is "Fat Tom," as he is known to his roommates, who murmurs appreciatively, "Big tree, real real real real big tree!" He is the cleanest boy in the cottage, for he loves to take baths. In the tub, he invariably bends himself double, straining to lick his penis, but is constantly frustrated because of his girth. Such severe disturbances led one house mother to describe the cottage as "the house of no return." For this despairing attitude she was dismissed by Montanari, who refuses to write off even these children as doomed. Despite their gross inadequacies, they have painted pictures of Frosty the snowman, and Rudolph the red-nosed reindeer, and pasted together colorful paper chains to adorn their cottage. A former resident of their cottage, a pleasant nineteen-year-old named Lenny, is employed part-time as an usher at the local movie theater while remaining in residence as a junior house father. "Most of these kids are luckier than me," he says. "They got folks to go home to for Christmas." Lenny was raised in an orphanage. . . .

At the cottage where Montanari's stepdaughter, Karen, resides, a party is in progress. One of the girls is going home, not merely for Christmas but for good, and the others have baked a celebration cake. One of their teachers, Miss Betty, who has five children of her own, drops by and invites the girls to come with her to the Royal Castle snack bar down the street, where she treats them all to ice cream and soda pop. On their return, they are greeted by Miss Kriss, another teacher—she is called a floating teacher because she "floats" about from group to group and from child to child as she is needed—and she plays Christmas carols on the recorder while they sing along. One girl, however, does not join in. This is Sheila, a plain-looking fourteen-year-old in a rumpled cotton dress, who sits in a corner weeping quietly to herself. She has learned that her aunt and uncle, who took her into their home when her own parents deserted her, will be away for the holiday, and is bitterly disappointed that she cannot be with them. She does not know that Monty has been trying to find some alternative to lift her spirits. Late in the afternoon he comes in, giving hugs to the girls, who rush to greet him, and then goes to Sheila and chucks her playfully under the chin. "I have some good news for you, honey," he tells her with a broad grin. "Tonight you're going to have Christmas dinner at my house with Karen, and then I'm going to drive you to the home of some folks you know very well and who are very anxious for you to spend the holidays with them." He mentions the name of a nearby family who are friends of the school and very fond of Sheila. When he asks, "How does that sound to you, honey?" she ceases to cry and starts smiling. . . .

At Christmas time, Montanari's office throbs with excitement. Children, parents and staff members come and go in a steady stream. Alver Louys surrenders her typing chores to a less over-burdened young assistant in order to deal more effectively with the visitors. Ruth Griffin takes parents aside to advise them how to handle their children while they are home for the holidays. When Monty is not dashing about from one cottage to the other, he is at his desk welcoming members of various civic groups who are arranging holiday festivities.

Monty's son, Gary, darkly handsome and tall as a ramrod, stops by his father's office to ask if there is anything he can do. "Sure," his father answers. "Go and play with the kids who can't go home for Christmas. Make them feel like they aren't missing much by spending Christmas here."

His daughter, Cissy, a bright and pretty girl with sparkling eyes and a pixie's smile, comes by to inquire her father's opin-ion on whether or not a box of cigars would make an appropri-ate gift for her grandfather. "A box? No," Monty shakes his head, "just buy him a small package of cigars, just to show the thought. You know my daddy. He'll appreciate the thought more than the cigars."

Quite suddenly, but not unexpectedly, "Santa's Caravan" ar-rives, bringing truckloads of toys contributed by interested local merchants, dispensed by several clowns and Santa himself. This highly thoughtful gesture is the brainchild of a man whose own life is dedicated to the needs of disturbed children. He is Abe Goldman, public-relations director of the Sunland Training Centers, and the joyous Caravan pays an annual visit not only to the Montanari School but to handicapped children clustered throughout Dade County. Monty's only regret is that "it all comes at one time, at Christmas, but the rest of the year, noth-ing."

The children gather together in the spacious yard outside Montanari's office to greet the Caravan. Teachers and house parents hustle about, toning down the overenthusiastic, nudging the spirits of the depressed. For every child there are several gifts: dolls and jump ropes for the little girls, blocks and bang-bang guns for the small boys, bubble bath and paste jewelry for the older girls, and baseball games and model airplanes for the bigger boys. But some youngsters stand apart, because they are terribly shy or because they are simply unable to comprehend. They are consoled and fortified by their teachers and house parents, who try to distract them from their withdrawal and to delight them with the shiny new playthings. Many of the children smash their toys within minutes of receiving them but they are immediately given replacements.

"I want a PT boat!" demands one small boy, a toy gun strapped to his waist, an oversize baseball cap all but covering his eyes, and his chin thrust out determinedly. This is Kevin, a devilish nine-year-old of very high intelligence whose brilliance is marred by childhood schizophrenia. He waves a letter proudly in Santa's face. It is a letter received from the late President John F. Kennedy, dated October 17, 1963, which he received in answer to his own laboriously lettered note. It reads: "Thank you for writing to me, Kevin. I understand that you would like to be in the Navy when you are older. I am sure that if you continue to work hard, you will be able to attain your ambitions. I am sorry that I am unable to accept your kind invitation to visit the Montanari school but I wish you and the other students a most successful year. I am sending you a short history of PT-109 and a photograph of PT-105, which is a sister boat of PT-109. Unfortunately, pictures of PT-109 are not available." After the neatly typed letter and his signature, the late President wrote in longhand: "Good luck!" More than anything else in the world, Kevin wanted to construct a model of a PT boat. Monty had bought him several such models but, each time, Kevin had destroyed them out of frustration at his inability to put them together successfully. Santa had been advised and Kevin was now presented with still another model along with a PT boat which was already fully constructed.

Soon after Santa's Caravan leaves, an eleven-year-old boy with rosy cheeks and a face like a cherub obtains admittance to Monty's office. He closes the door tightly behind him, stares at Monty for a few seconds, then suddenly rushes over to him and begins to tear at his shirt.

"Billy!" exclaims the startled Montanari as he tries to hold

off the boy. "What are you trying to do? Settle down now!"
But Billy disregards him and continues to tear at Monty's
clothes, panting, "I'm gonna take everything off you, Monty, so
I can get out of here and run back home for Christmas. Without
no clothes, you won't be able to run after me because you'll be
naked."

Montanari conceals his surprise at the boy's audacity, pins his
arms to his sides and calms him down. After the child returns
to his cottage, Montanari explains, "I just couldn't tell Billy that
the reason he wasn't going home was because his parents didn't
want him. I made all kinds of excuses to him to cover up the
real reason. Oh, hell, I could have insisted that his parents
take him for the holiday but I was afraid they'd be so mean to
him that it would do him more harm than good. So I took the
blame for Billy's not going home and that's why this little son
of a gun comes in here, trying to rip the clothes off my back so
that he can run home and I can't run after him. He's a very
shrewd little boy."

Not long after Christmas, Billy revealed the true extent of his
cleverness in a quite remarkable way. He rigged up a long wire,
connected one end to a regular electric plug and the other to the
metal gate of the play yard outside his cottage. When he heard
that one of his classmates, a habitual runaway, was making
ready to run again, he shoved the plug into an outlet on the
porch of his cottage, thus electrifying the metal gate. When his
classmate attempted to climb the gate after dinner, as Billy expected he would, the boy received a sharp jolt of electricity,
harmless but with enough power behind it to send him sprawling
backward in the grass.

Elated by the success of his enterprise, Billy proudly exclaimed
to the astonished staff members who came rushing to the scene,
"See what I done for you? I kept him from running away. Now
I can't go home and neither can he. And you don't have to go
out lookin' for him because he didn't go nowhere. Ain't you all
proud of me?"

Montanari still shakes his head with disbelief as he recalls
the incident. "I've been around such kids too long to be surprised by anything," he says, "but this thing Billy did startled

the hell out of me. When word got around, right away I was asked why I didn't do research to find out why a kid does things like this and how he can be so smart when he's supposed to be so disturbed. Well, I'm not interested in research. I don't have the time to try to figure out exactly why a child acts this way or that. All I want to do is get these kids out of here, back to society and able to get along to the best of their ability. We haven't got time to fool around, you see. I just try to get these kids to a point where we think we have a finger in the goddamn dike. Because if I pull out my finger for even a minute, we're all going to drown. Clever as Billy is, it won't help him if we know why he wired the fence—I mean the real deeply buried reason why. It will help him more if we can give him new ways to use his cleverness and build up his ego to the point where he can return home and be able to put up with frustration."

In Montanari's opinion, psychiatry is not always enough nor is it always necessary. But as more children were entered in the school and the need to hasten their recovery became pressing, he engaged more professional consultants to expedite diagnostic evaluations and to make therapy available when called for, satisfying critics who continued to object to his own lack of academic qualification despite his high degree of success.

Since his was a private enterprise, professionals would not contribute their services or reduce their customary fees even on behalf of nonpaying children, so he employed them, at first, on an hourly basis.

In 1961, he went all out and engaged as director of psychological services Dr. William P. Albaugh, a good-humored, easygoing clinical psychologist who was a diplomate of the American Psychological Association and who had acquired a wealth of experience working with disturbed children at several public and private agencies.

"Monty was always a controversial figure," chuckles Dr. Albaugh, "and there was always a lot of resistance to him in the field. But I saw that he was taking a very professional approach to the task of dealing with emotionally disturbed children and saw that some professionals were trying to take advantage of him, wanting to lend him the use of their names for a fee without doing anything to deserve it. Well, Monty isn't the sort of man who'll pay for names to put on his letterhead. He wants people who will work with his kids. I felt pretty stimulated by the challenge, so I took the job."

Soon afterward, Montanari engaged Dr. Evan Katz, a child psychiatrist and former director of the Dade County Child Guidance Clinic, as director of psychiatric services. "His approach impressed me," says Dr. Katz, "because I could see how it became possible to reach many unreachable children, using the techniques that he had pioneered, and to reach more of them by using a staff of skilled lay people working under professional supervision. I became another resource for Monty to draw on."

More recently, Montanari added a full-time psychometrician, Marjorie Bayes, to administer psychological tests right on the premises. An attractive, soft-spoken young woman, she possesses an MA in psychology and is keenly observant. She has to be, for an important ingredient of the testing procedure is the perceptive observation of a child's total behavior.

During a typical testing session, she may note that the youngster, in writing down his responses to her questions, is scrawling to the very edges of the paper. When he is asked why, he explains, "It's a waste of money to throw away paper unused." This need to save leads to the discovery that the child is fearful of there not being enough money in his home. With further encouragement, he reveals how he associates saving not only with money, but with people, the saving of people. "Lots of times," he blurts out, "I dream about swimming in the ocean and I get so tired, I want to be saved so's I won't be eaten by a great big fish." Now it is he himself who wishes to be saved. By this indirect route, he has illuminated to the perceptive psychometrician his repressed feelings of anxiety.

Some tests are purely oral. A young girl may be asked to complete the statement: "Lemons are sour but sugar is . . .?" The unexpected reply may be: "For coffee." She may be asked directly: "What should you do when you cut your finger?" And the unexpected reply may be: "Make it bleed." These are labeled "inappropriate responses" and serve to demonstrate the child's lack of touch with reality.

Simple word-association tests are standard practice and used frequently as an adjunct to other more complicated techniques. A hyperactive seven-year-old bouncing about the clinic office going "Bang bang!" with a toy gun during the testing session is asked to define the single word "puddle." He stamps his feet, jumps about, knits his brows reflectively and finally replies, "Puddle puddle puddle . . . when it rains, you're in a puddle."

"Law? How about law?"

"Law law law . . . it means . . . it means . . . you don't be in a puddle!"

Then the boy is shown cards with variously shaped inkblots on them—the classic Rorschach test—and asked, "What do you see here?"

With his little finger, he traces imaginary lines across the inkblot and replies earnestly, "Here's the woods . . . and here is dubbydie . . . oh yes, he will dubbydie . . . from the butterfly in the woods . . . then the man will kill the bear . . . oh, this is things . . . cats fighting . . . and here is the butterfly . . . and here is the child . . . that there's a bear . . . this is what it shall be, oh yes . . . the butterfly shall kill the child and he will dubbydie."

Here are the elements of childhood schizophrenia. In the testing experience, the tangible intangibles that comprise mental disturbance take grotesque shape and become exposed.

"These tests rely on scientific measurement," Miss Bayes points out, "whereas Monty relies on a combination of intuition and experience. He will often say to me, 'I think this child is retarded as well as autistic but I'd like you to check on this.' Nine times out of ten, his diagnosis is accurate. The tests validate his original suspicions. When it comes out that he is wrong, he accepts the test results. But, in all frankness, tests are not infallible, either. After teachers and house parents have worked closely with a child, for example, they may find that the test results have overstated the severity of the child's emotional problem."

Montanari chuckles at this observation, "You see, you can't trust science any more than you can trust me."

In this connection, Dr. Howard Engle, who is Montanari's consultant on neurological problems, adds, "Monty doesn't simply take the word of a psychologist or psychiatrist that a child is untreatable. The so-called hopeless child is rejected from the Clinical School only after a reasonable trial period. As long as Monty can see the slightest chance for improvement, the child stays. This kind of stubborn determination is like a breath of fresh air in this field."

To illustrate how the lay staff and the professional staff work together, Montanari pulls out the file on Jeff Rothman, explaining, "This is a boy who likes to run. As soon as a teacher, a house parent or one of my supervisors suspects that Jeff is getting ready to run away, word is passed along to me. My first step, then, is to talk to the boy as soon as possible to see if I can't head off this urge."

Here is a word-for-word transcript of such a conversation. It takes place in Montanari's office at eight o'clock in the morning. Jeff, a scrawny boy, stands hesitantly in the doorway, his hands thrust deep into the pockets of his chinos, his nervousness apparent. He blinks his eyes and twitches his nose continuously.

"Well, come on in, Jeff," says Monty affably, waving the boy to a chair beside his desk. "Go on, sit down."

Still hesitant, his eyes still blinking, his nose still twitching, Jeff finally moves toward the chair and sits down stiffly. He glares at Monty with evident disdain and says, "I don't like to see you in a suit."

"Why? Why don't you like to see me in a suit?"

"You don't look so hot."

Monty laughs. "I don't look so hot? How do you want me to look—cool, man, cool?"

Jeff does not answer. His defenses are up. "Well, OK, I'm here," he says sullenly. "What'd you wanna see me about?"

"Tell me, son," replies Monty, avoiding the main issue, "why did you call your house mother, Miss Jane, a big cow yesterday at lunchtime, hm?"

"Because I was pissed off."

"Why were you pissed off?"

"There were little white specks in my tomato juice, that's why."

"Now, Jeff, you know that was only some powdered sugar that dropped in from the cornflakes. Did Miss Jane punish you?"

"No."

"Did you think she would?"

"Yeah."

"If she had, what would you have done?"

"I'd 've run away, that's what, and you know it."

Monty does not answer. He allows the boy to squirm a bit, then says, "Listen, Jeff, are you mad at Miss Jane?"

"No."

"Are you mad at somebody else?" No answer. "At yourself?" Still no answer. "Maybe you're mad at me, Jeff. Would you like to take a poke at me?" He sticks out his stomach and spreads his hands wide, leaving himself vulnerable. "Go ahead, Jeff. If it'll make you feel better, take a good hard sock at me."

The brazen invitation seems to frighten the boy. He puts his head down and begins to twitch violently.

"Settle down, Jeff," says Monty, his voice soft and soothing. "Would you like to talk to Dr. Katz or Dr. Albaugh?"

"I hate those guys," Jeff retorts angrily. "I won't say nothin' to them. I hate 'em almost as much as I hate this place. I wanna go home. Lemme go home, Monty, please, lemme go home."

"Now, Jeff, you do go home most weekends, you know that. But your mama tells me you don't behave yourself too well, you act up, and if she says for you to stop, you run away."

Jeff fidgets uncomfortably, remaining silent. Then, in a peevish tone, he complains, "Aw, listen, Monty, she was supposed to meet me down at the corner the other day and take me out with her for a while, but she never showed up."

"She was? I didn't know about that."

"Well, I wrote her a letter to meet me. I didn't tell anybody about it. Maybe she never got it."

Monty removes his glasses and twirls them between his fingers. It is a ploy, to distract Jeff and to give himself time to think. After a half minute or so, he replaces the glasses, leans forward and says, "You know, Jeff, what I think you should do? I think you should go back to your cottage after class today and write another letter to your mama. Write her a nice long letter. Tell her about that wooden butterfly you cut out on the jigsaw in shop, and about that softball game where you drove home a run. She likes to hear about such things. You write her a nice long letter all about the things you've been doing here and I'll see to it personally that this time she gets it. OK?"

Jeff's face brightens. His twitching subsides a bit. Eagerly, he asks, "After I write the letter, can I have permission to walk around by myself and visit some of the other boys?"

"Yeah, if you don't act like a jackass." Monty grins. "Now go on back to class, Jeff."

Later, commenting on this dialogue, Montanari says, "The dynamics of this particular case—what I just did may not make a goddamned bit of sense to anybody else, but it does to me. I channeled something negative into something positive, you see. I resolved the crisis for the next twenty-four hours. It's a temporary solution, sure, but it's better than nothing. At least I'm controlling him. He wants to be controlled, you see, he wants to be stopped from running. But I can't just put limits on him and say, 'This is how far you can go, you little smart alec, from here to the end of the hall and no farther.' He'll spit in my face if I try to do that. I have to put limits on him without closing the door on him. It's hard to explain just how far you can let this boy go before you put your foot down. You just have to feel it. There aren't any pat answers."

In an attempt to find a more permanent solution to Jeff's difficulty, Montanari sets up a staff meeting with Ruth Griffin, his assistant; David Colton, the boy's house father; Mrs. Elinor Turner, the boy's caseworker; Dr. Alberto de la Torre, the Clinical School's special psychiatric consultant; and Dr. Albaugh, serving as chairman. Promptly at three, they join Montanari in the one-story stucco building which houses the school's clinical facility.

Rarely, if ever, are the intimate workings of a treatment center for disturbed children so clearly and dramatically revealed to the outsider. But here is a precise documentation of what transpired at this meeting. . . .

X

"WE ARE TALKING VERY INFORMALLY today," begins Dr. Albaugh. "We have to decide if Jeff Rothman is a boy we can help and, if so, how to do this as quickly as possible. Jeff has been here in residence almost three months. He is eleven and a half years old and is a chronic runaway. That's his basic pattern."

"No overt delinquency?" asks Dr. de la Torre, an extraordinarily alert, self-assured man with a pleasantly efficient manner.

"Not really," Dr. Albaugh replies. "Jeff is a very nervous boy and can be a holy terror at times, but has no delinquent pattern. He's the oldest of five children and seems to be the only one who's become a problem. The family moved to Miami from New Jersey about a year ago and, in both places, Jeff played truant from school more times than he attended classes. When he did show up, he acted up a great deal and had to be dismissed."

"What happens with this boy," Monty interjects, "is that he starts out in jest, smart-alecky, you see, and then it snowballs and builds up and up until he can't stop. He gets wild. Then the minute you put your foot down, he runs away."

"He's very sensitive," adds Ruth Griffin. "One time, his teacher took his class on a visit to a farm and said to the boys, 'Look, look at the pigs.' Well, Jeff became terribly indignant and cussed out his teacher for calling them pigs. He said it was disrespectful and their feelings would be hurt."

There is a smattering of laughter and Dr. de la Torre asks, "He saw nothing funny in that remark?"

"Not at all. In fact, he became more and more outraged as the day wore on. And that evening, he ran away."

There is a slight pause and then Dr. de la Torre speaks. "Well, my immediate reaction, in terms of the degree of control that this child has, is that I think very probably he has a failure in maturation, the primary process breakthrough. He has to have what he wants when he wants it. He has to be right even when he is being ridiculous. I'm just speculating, but does the psychological substantiate this, Bill?"

"Yes, it does," agrees Dr. Albaugh. "His responses were primitive in the Rorschach given him at Jackson Memorial Hospital some months ago. Incidentally, he ran away from there while he was under observation. He took a few squares of Celotex soundproofing from the ceiling, climbed through to the next floor, somehow got to another ward, found an open door and went home."

"Tell me more about the Rorschach."

"His reaction to the inkblots was pure color. He didn't take into consideration the form of the blots."

"Usually, we interpret this to mean that such a child's responses are automatic and uncontrolled. That seems to fit in with this boy."

"His other test responses show a great deal of latent hostility as well. Here, take a look at these drawings he made."

Jeff's drawings are passed around. Most show stick figures hanging by their necks from scaffolds and being stabbed by other stick figures. One picture depicts two women dismembering a body. Red crayon to indicate the flow of blood is everywhere.

"There seems to be something more here," notes Dr. de la Torre. "See in this drawing how he has a small boy tied to a post and with a free hand this boy is trying to light a fire at his feet. But next to it is written: 'Help me, sombody, help me!' This seems to suggest that Jeff is pleading for controls, that he has this desire to harm himself but is hoping for someone to keep him from doing things that will hurt him."

"Well, when I set limits, they've been pretty successful," volunteers Monty. "I can resolve a crisis for the time being this way. But what bothers me about this boy is that he remains likable even when he's fighting you."

"This kind of behavioral evidence would substantiate the possibility that he is really pleading for controls. Have you tried giving him any kind of therapy, Bill?" Dr. de la Torre asks.

Dr. Albaugh shakes his head. "I didn't want to commit myself to it or commit him to it," he says, "until circumstances were right for a reasonable chance of success. Jeff is a bright child. His IQ is, at the very least, 112. But at this moment, the only one he responds to is Monty."

Pondering this information, Dr. de la Torre comments, "You know, before we can decide how much freedom this boy can take and what limits we can impose, we have to decide what to do about his parents. It is significant that he seems to want to run home, then as soon as he arrives there, to run away again."

"That's right," Monty agrees. "Every time he goes home, it's like reopening an old wound. I can sympathize with his parents. I know that Jeff is uncooperative at home and that having such a child around can be like rubbing sandpaper on raw nerves. But this boy's mama tries to saddle him with a bunch of dos and don'ts that normal kids conform to. Jeff's too disturbed for that sort of thing. He can't conform."

"I have a letter here," Ruth Griffin interjects, "that Jeff's mother wrote to the boy. It's pretty typical of all her letters. I'd just like to read one part: 'You are here on earth to do your share to add to the world's happiness, not to its trouble, for in order to be loved, you must be deserving of it.' Right after reading this letter, Jeff tried to run away."

Mrs. Turner, the caseworker, who has so far remained silent, suddenly speaks up. "I have found these parents to be very uncooperative. They beg Monty to send Jeff home on visits more often, but I have the feeling that they don't really want him around. I know for a fact that the other children tease him unmercifully. I was there and saw them do so, and the mother didn't interfere in any way."

"She cries to me all the time," adds Monty, "like she's very concerned. But she really considers this boy some kind of animal, a thorn in her side. This week, for example, Jeff wrote and asked her to meet him one afternoon and she never showed up or even bothered to answer his letter."

"You think, then, that she is in a way inviting him to run away?" asks Dr. de la Torre. "Encouraging him to get lost somewhere, perhaps, to be rid of him because of her own subconscious conflicts?"

"I'm no authority on this woman's subconscious conflicts," answers Monty with a shy grin. "I do think that she does have some love for this child, some maternal feeling for him in her own sick way. But from everything she's told me, and from what Jeff has told me, I don't think she has very much love of any kind for her husband."

"That's so," responds Mrs. Turner. "I sensed Mr. and Mrs. Rothman's dislike for each other every time I visited their home. She especially seemed to be full of hate and anger."

Dr. de la Torre nods his head, puckers his lips thoughtfully, then says, "It is possible that this boy is not so impulsive as I had suggested earlier, but that he is playing out his mother's fantasy of getting rid of this husband she does not like. What sort of man is he?"

"I don't know for sure," replies Monty. "He never comes around. But I do know that he is always going out by himself. His wife told me that he likes to go dancing and that she doesn't care for dancing, so he goes out alone."

"Hmmmm," muses Dr. de la Torre. "This suggests another possibility, that Jeff is identifying with his father. In other words, if the father is the one who wants to run away from the home situation and somehow conveys this message to Jeff, the boy could do it, run away in place of the father."

For the first time, David Colton, Jeff's house father, speaks up. "I met Mr. Rothman once," he says. "It was a week or so ago when I brought Jeff to Miami to spend a day with his father. Mr. Rothman tried to give Jeff a peck on the cheek and the boy pulled away from him. I don't know if this was because Jeff is afraid to display affection or because he dislikes his dad, or because he's afraid of him. I don't know, but I'd like to add another observation, if I may. I've noticed that when kids pick on Jeff, he doesn't fight back. He just runs the other way."

Monty nods his head vigorously. "That's right," he says. "Jeff talks big but won't fight. I think if he could become more aggressive and learn to follow through when somebody bugs him, it would be healing. He'd stop running."

For a minute or so, there is a lull in the conversation. Then Dr. de la Torre says, "You know, I am beginning to feel that this child's problem is that he is fundamentally a neglected child, that nobody ever helped him to develop inner controls because his mother is always too busy loving her other kids and his father is always too busy avoiding the mother and probably all the kids."

"Go a step further," suggests Monty. "Jeff wants to be an ordinary human being like everybody else but knows that his mama, his daddy, his brothers and sisters all think he's an oddball. Maybe that's why he seems to trust me more than anyone else, because he figures I'm an oddball, too; I don't know."

Everyone laughs and Dr. de la Torre says enthusiastically, "I think certain things stand out pretty clearly now. First, this is a boy whom we can help. Second, all of us—teachers, house parents, everyone—must make him understand that we are the boss, because this boy needs this kind of reassurance. Third, we have to let our own intuitive grasp of each situation dictate when we can relent and when we must clamp down, for unfortunately there is no scientific gauge to measure this. But we must be careful not to give Jeff too much freedom too quickly. This could be dangerous."

"We will put limits on him," offers Monty, "but we will not close the door on him."

"Exactly," replies Dr. de la Torre, and the others murmur agreement.

Monty's earlier contention has been confirmed. He has kept in step with professional opinion. This is highly meaningful to him because, despite his limited formal training, he considers himself fully qualified as a professional person by virtue of his experience in the field and his natural ability to comprehend the bizarre behavior of a disturbed child.

As guest speaker at a recent conference on emotionally disturbed children, sponsored by the Southern Regional Education Board at Tallahassee, he said, "We have a responsibility as professionals working with disturbed children to learn basic skills and techniques. But this in itself is not enough in view of the tremendous demands and needs imposed by the numbers of children involved. We must not be afraid to venture and pioneer in new areas."

He refuses to stand at a respectable professional distance from a child who needs help. He cuts across boundaries that separate therapist from patient and becomes involved. "I'm not a doctor. I'm a teacher, an educator—perhaps a better word is reeducator—and in order to reeducate an emotionally damaged youngster, I have to get inside that youngster's mind. I have to think the way a child thinks, you see."

He does more than simply go down to the child's level. In order to establish healthy controls, he becomes a part of the child's sickness. When asked if there was any danger of his becoming contaminated, he replied, "The 'hoodlum priest' wasn't contaminated. You have to know when to get involved and when to get uninvolved."

Although Montanari has broadened his base of operations to include more specialists of high academic qualification, he remains skeptical about the value of purely formal training which too often leads to academic rigidity. He never overlooks an opportunity to twit his colleagues on the subject.

Once, when a prominent psychoanalyst visited the Clinical School, he noticed that Monty liked to chew on the frames of his eyeglasses and asked him, with the ghost of a smirk, why he did so. "I don't know," Monty laughed, "I just like to chew on them, that's all. But I'm sure it's a psychiatric thing. Maybe I'm masturbating, hm? Anyway, it doesn't bother me. But what I want to know is: why does it bother *you?*"

Montanari continues to startle those who cannot understand him or who will not take the trouble to try.

When Dr. William Curtis Adams, former medical director of the Variety Children's Hospital in Miami, advised the American Child Guidance Foundation that Montanari had "obtained results with emotionally disturbed children that would be difficult to duplicate in either time or cost," and pleaded for the Foundation's backing to help obtain financial assistance for Monty from the National Institute of Health "or some other major granting body," he met with snickers for his trouble.

When Dr. Lloyd J. Borstelmann, associate professor of psychology and psychiatry at Duke University, proposed Monty as the member of a panel debating new methods in treating the emotionally disturbed child, the highly esteemed Society for Research in Child Development—sponsored by the University of Minnesota—rejected him as "too applied," suggesting that Monty had been too successful in working with disturbed children to contribute very much to a theoretical discussion on the subject. An appalled Dr. Borstelmann replied, "I would hope that the Society is both stable and secure enough not only to tolerate, but to welcome the opportunity to hear from an occasional maverick whose actions may open new vistas for our study." But the answer from the ivory tower of the pious professionals remained a resounding *no*.

Monty finds a far more favorable reception among young people, undergraduates of colleges like Smith, Antioch and Miami University, who frequently visit the school and often serve as assistant teachers and house parents in order to obtain firsthand experience in the fields of psychology and social work. They are encouraged to put down their impressions, and Monty says, "These young people don't pull their punches. They say what they mean and I welcome their criticism. They're young and fresh and filled up to here with wonderful ideals. When they see something they don't like, in my methods or my staff or in me, I pay attention. I may not always agree but it gives me a chance to take a second look around."

A recent visit by the senior psychology class of Florida Atlantic University occasioned these comments: "I can see where empathy and rapport with troubled children is as vital as a university degree. . . ." "The permissive atmosphere which prevailed on the entire school grounds was refreshing and enlightening. Adult control and supervision were so subtly applied that at times it seemed to be almost nonexistent. . . ." "Although the director appeared at times to be unprofessional in language and manner, it was obvious that he was extremely well-liked by the children and seems to know exactly what he is doing. It is a shame if his critics are misled by his salty language."

Among the unfavorable comments, this one stands out: "This place left me cold. I wonder what magic is worked here. The school is spread out over several blocks. The teachers seem to require no formal training, no basic psychology or educational courses, only some vague qualifications set forth by Mr. Montanari such as understanding and compassion. They reminded me of Bible school recruits."

Controversial though he may be, Monty has received professional recognition from such highly regarded sources as the International Council for Exceptional Children, the American Association on Mental Deficiency, the National Association for Retarded Children and the Florida Psychiatric Association. In 1964, he received the annual Distinguished Service Award from his alma mater, Western Carolina College, in honor of his accomplishments. The citation read: "His entire career has been marked by those ideal qualities of selflessness which place the truly dedicated teacher apart from all others. His is the inquiring, questioning mind that leads one away from the 'beaten track' into avenues of decision, action and service without regard to whether his course is the conventional one."

Montanari's dramatic disregard for convention, coupled with his remarkable achievements with severely disturbed children, made good copy and attracted the attention of prominent national publications. Some of the stories were reprinted in translations, and the Clinical School became deluged by letters in a variety of languages.

An amusing and revealing side note to this sudden splash of notoriety is provided by an anecdote concerning the reaction of Monty's father. When the elder Montanari was shown his son's photograph in a well-known magazine, he stared at it for a long while, finally remarking with pleasure and astonishment, "You know, when you look at my boy's picture, he looks so very smart!"

None of these emblems of success, however, impressed Montanari's neighbors in Deer Park. Since their defeat in 1959, when they had attempted to close the school on a zoning charge, they had remained silent, nursing their hurt and quietly rebuilding their forces. Six years later they struck out again.

Early in 1965, the city of Hialeah made national headlines. Its population of approximately 85,000 was staging a gala week-long celebration to commemorate the fortieth anniversary of the world-famous Hialeah Race Course. Festivities ranged from a "haute couture" fashion show to the crowning of a buxom local lass as "Miss Hialeah."

For forty days and nights, the very best people—the cream of American high society, industry, theater and politics—flocked to Hialeah to watch the horses run at what many observers have called the most beautiful of all racetracks. Even the dignified *New York Times* considered the occasion memorable enough to merit a full page of photographs in its Sunday edition.

Regrettably, none of these influential people, many of whom are publicly credited with a lively interest in the less fortunate, troubled themselves to read the front pages of the local newspapers. If they had, they would have discovered that there was another race being run a mere mile away from the Hialeah track. The contenders here were not horses, but disturbed children. The purse was not a matter of dollars and cents, but the opportunity to embrace life as total human beings.

This was the setting for Montanari's new confrontation with his Deer Park neighbors and the Hialeah City Council. This time he was accused of operating "both a private and public nuisance." The new demand to revoke Montanari's occupational license in Deer Park was based on a local ordinance that specified the importance of preserving the public health by preventing or removing "any accumulation of trash, filth or other matter."

Monty was furious. "Now they're equating my kids with garbage!" he exclaimed to reporters. "Some of my neighbors think Deer Park is a second Coral Gables but, if you look around, you'll see a hamburger stand right outside our door. They want me out but they won't buy me out and they won't find another place for me to go. But every time a disturbance is created, they look at my children. They've harassed me at all hours. One day, a neighbor's child stood outside our fence and threw lighted firecrackers into the yard, scaring my kids half to death. And did anybody call that child a nuisance? Hell, no, because that child is not disturbed, he's just a normal kid out having a good time!"

Word of this new assault against Monty spread quickly. The local newspapers, the radio and television stations ran editorials in his behalf. Hialeah's collective conscience, private, public and professional, became aroused.

Juvenile Court Judge Ben J. Sheppard beseeched the City Council by letter. "More and more as the years go by," he wrote, "the slogan of those who work with disturbed children has been 'Send them to Monty's.' Mr. Montanari has taken an uncounted number of children off our hands and has rehabilitated them so that they could return to the normal school environment and behave in an acceptable manner. I feel that not enough recognition has been given to Mr. Montanari and his school. I feel that he should be the recipient of much help and praise."

A prominent citizen, unknown to Montanari, adressed a moving letter to each member of the City Council. "It is amazing, in this day and age," he wrote, "that we must be compelled to fight so many people in order to do the things which they themselves should be helping us to accomplish. Many years ago, when Bishop Sheil, the founder of the Catholic Youth Organization, was a priest, he served as prison chaplain. Pursuing his duties as chaplain, he approached a young murderer who was about to be executed for his crime. He asked the boy, 'Son, is there anything I can do for you?' The boy looked at him with anguished eyes and replied, 'Father, why do they wait until there is a rope around my neck before they try to do something for me?' "

Hialeah's affable mayor, Henry Milander, whose tenure in office exceeds two decades, said of Montanari, "I helped him get in there on a variance report to see what he could do, and he kept on growing, expanding. Then some of the neighbors got real mad about it, you know, but I told them he's been there and you can't change it now. It's just like before the zoning law went into effect and I had a meat market in the heart of the residential section. They couldn't put me out because of a 'grand-father club claim.' You couldn't say he's really operating a business. I doubt if there's a court in the world that would."

Mayor Milander revealed that he had received a personal letter from Florida's governor, Haydon Burns, who pointed out that there was a waiting list of 1,700 children for admittance to the five Sunland Training Centers for handicapped children. The governor urged city authorities to consider such facts when dealing with the complaint against Montanari, pleading, "I earnestly request the attempt to close this institution be denied."

William H. Mapoles, director of the Sunland Training Centers, replying to a letter from a Hialeah woman who expressed anxiety about the possibility that the Montanari School would be shut down, referred to the school as "a critically needed facility" and assured the woman "that Governor Burns, and other interested officials in the State, have or will intervene for these unfortunate children who cannot speak for themselves."

And William H. Lockward, president of the Hialeah City Council, said of Montanari prior to the hearing, "Everybody feels he does a terrific job. They need this type of thing to help kids. This is what Florida and most of the other states are lacking."

But, unfortunately, politics often leaves reason behind. The new attack by the Deer Park Homeowners' Association was launched against the eighteen young boys in residence and the forty other students who attended classes at the Deer Park facility. The public hearing before Hialeah's City Council took place, as scheduled, on February 16, 1965, in a large, gloomy room which was so crowded with participants and spectators that many had to stand through the entire proceedings. Mr. Lockward presided. Six fellow councilmen and the mayor were also in attendance. At precisely 7:30 P.M. on a balmy Tuesday evening, City Attorney Ralph F. Miles gave his opening remarks in the case against Montanari.

For more than three hours, eleven residents of Deer Park denounced Monty's children for trespassing, for being noisy and for using profanity. In spite of the intensity with which they voiced their denunciation, they could not document a single charge. Under cross-examination, most admitted that they had never previously registered a complaint with Montanari.

By inference, they made clear that they considered their own children to be models of perfect behavior who never raised their voices, never talked back, never got into childish mischief, never had nightmares, never climbed trees, never threw things, never left litter lying about, never received nor deserved any punishment whatever, never lied, never became upset and never teased other children.

At 11:00 P.M., Montanari's chief legal counsel, State Senator Robert M. Haverfield, began calling the first of eleven witnesses to the stand. These included state representatives, child psychiatrists, mental-health authorities, a juvenile-court judge, the county's chief probation officer, parents of children attending the school and Monty himself.

Jack V. Blanton, chief probation officer of the Dade County Juvenile Court for eighteen years, testified that he had worked closely with Montanari for nine years and knew nothing of the "screaming, escaping, profanity" about which the homeowners complained. "No, we've received no complaints about the school," he said, and suggested that he would have been one of the first to know if any such complaints had been registered. He indicated that at least twenty neighborhood children were accepted by Monty each year and remarked dryly, "Oh, yes, we have big strong cells and big strong men to quiet them down and isolate them from the others—but this school rehabilitates them, makes them whole again. We need more of these facilities, not less."

The mother of an eight-year-old boy in residence at the Clinical School for a year testified that her son was now able to attend Hialeah Elementary Public School. She spoke highly of Monty's methods of building confidence in children, one of which is to send them on little errands in the neighborhood. "My little boy, like so many other youngsters, runs everywhere he goes," she related. "One day he went running down the street on an errand to get three Cokes and the youngsters across the street"—(whose mother had testified earlier to children "escaping" from the school)—"shouted, 'There's one of those crazy Montanari kids!

Let's get him!' And they did. My son was kicked in the stomach, had his head banged on the sidewalk and was beaten badly."

Dr. Alan A. Lipton, a psychiatrist and chairman of the executive committee of the Dade County Commission on Youth, was questioned by one of the councilmen as to whether he would prefer to have his family reside next door to the Montanari facility or a public school, and he replied, "I know something of the public schools and the juvenile-delinquency rate. I'd much rather have my home and family next to the Montanari School." He pointed out that a bad child, whether normal or disturbed, is still a bad child, and that some of the very best-behaved children are frequently the sickest.

When Dr. Richard Emerson, director of the Dade County Child Guidance Clinic, was asked how it would affect children living next door, he answered, "Only if the parents reflect anxiety and a lack of understanding will their children pick it up and in turn reflect it in their attitudes and behavior toward the youngsters of the Montanari School."

This was corroborated by Dr. Evan Katz, Monty's psychiatric director, who emphasized that "emotional illness is not a measure of behavioral disturbance."

It was almost 1:00 A.M. when Senator Haverfield called his eleventh and final witness to the stand. The weary audience suddenly came alive. A stir of excitement ran through the room. For the witness was Monty himself.

He was tired. He would have preferred to postpone his appearance until the following morning but the City Council ruled against it, insisting that the hearing be concluded in a single session regardless of the late hour.

With characteristic patience, Montanari replied to each count raised against him. He made clear the point that while he was grateful to the City of Hialeah for all the kindnesses extended to the children in his care, he would not cease to fight for the rights of these children if they were placed in jeopardy.

"Gentlemen," he addressed the councilmen and the mayor, "these children aren't incarcerated. They don't escape from anywhere. There are no locked doors. Perhaps they do run into neighbors' yards, sure, but the children in the neighborhood go through our yard and we don't complain. We like them. But let it be my children . . ."

His voice trailed off in a rare moment of impatience. Then he regained his composure and continued. "Someone stole a car and the neighbors said it was one of my boys," he said, "but it turned out he was in Tampa at the time. The neighbors say my children curse but so do the other children. Did you ever hear boys who didn't curse at one time or another? Thirty of my children go to public school. I keep closer supervision on them than many parents and I've never lost a child."

He shifted around in his chair and looked directly at his accusers. "This is no indictment against me," he said quietly. "They all love *me*. It's my children they don't like. Well, if you're nice to children, they'll be nice to you. They love affection. Kids react as you treat them."

Suddenly he turned again and his eyes swept over the members of the City Council. "Some of these kids," he said, "are your kids, and I can document it." He paused for a moment, then continued, "Give a child an ounce of love and you'll get more in return. But don't tell them they're crazy or that they don't belong here. If you do, I'll expect them to curse you—or I will if they don't!"

At 1:45 A.M., the members of City Council recessed to arrive at a decision. A half hour later they reconvened to give their verdict. President Lockward announced that a majority of the Council had decided that "the Montanari Clinical School serves a critical need . . . and the City has no desire to limit the overall operation," but that in their opinion the Deer Park facility "does constitute a public and private nuisance to the residents in that immediate area, depriving them of a peaceable enjoyment of their property."

Monty was given until October 1, 1965, to vacate the premises, and his attorney's request for a poll of the Council's vote was denied.

The following day, the *Miami News* published a front-page editorial which began: "Psychiatry at midnight may have been too much for the weary members of the City Council or the audience to comprehend." In the same edition, Jack Kassewitz, chief editorial writer for the paper, wrote a scathing column titled "Trial by Neighborhood."

Referring to the hysteria that once drove citizens to burn "witches" in Salem, Massachusetts, he went on to say, "We thought such town-hall trials had long ago gone by the boards until his neighbors set upon A. J. Montanari before the Hialeah City Council." He pointed out that "one of the councilmen who voted against the educator had a nephew in Monty's home for nine months. Today the child is back home with his parents and considered perfectly normal." He made reference to "the back-yard gossip and opinion, and not always fact" that overruled the more informed opinion supporting Montanari, and concluded, "The entire evening leaves an observer with the impression that Montanari's nosy neighbors, aided and abetted by the Hialeah Council, won't stop with one school."

Mr. Kassewitz' warning is beginning to bear fruit. The city tax collector has already given Montanari notice that, henceforth, the cost of renewal of his occupational licenses for his other locations will be doubled, and has reclassified his facilities from "Clinical School and Foster Home" to "Child Boarding Home." Montanari is fighting to alter such reclassification, which he considers improper, inaccurate and "just a means of invoking zoning violations against me."

At this writing, the October 1 deadline has come and gone but the decision against Montanari has not been invoked. He has made no effort to move and has threatened that "if they come to make me move, I'll take the kids to City Hall. I'll hold classes there and I'll bunk the kids there."

Official action against Montanari was postponed for ninety days after one councilman admitted to reporters, "Before we lock his door, we'd better find a suitable place for him to move. We promised him that and we haven't done our part."

A special Citizens Committee was organized for this purpose but Monty scoffed, "They're only trying to pacify me. It's just local politics. There's an election coming up and they know I have public opinion on my side. I intend to take this out of local politics to the courts and make it strictly a legal battle. If I have to, I'll take it all the way up to the Supreme Court."

It is interesting to note that, on the heels of their ruling against Montanari, the same City Council passed an ordinance allowing a dog-grooming establishment to do business in a similarly zoned residential area.

It is interesting, also, to note the comment of a Deer Park homeowner who maintains that he is "neutral" but whose wife was one of the eleven witnesses who testified so truculently against the children attending the school. When asked what he thought his neighbors would do with the school facility should the children be forced out, he replied enthusiastically, "They'd have a place for their country club, they could make a country club of it."

The country club may yet become a reality and put fifty well-adjusted grownups on the golf course instead of putting as many emotionally disenfranchised youngsters on the long road back to life. But this is only conjecture. The battle is destined to continue for some time. Montanari is not easily thwarted. He thrives on challenges that tax his resourcefulness.

Already, he has written a letter which has received wide circulation in both popular and professional journals, in which he states:

I am beginning to wonder if we are paying anything more than lip service to America's troubled children. We are told that only a handful of the most troubled kids are getting any help and learn from the U.S. Joint Commission on Mental Illness and Health that "the job to be done throughout the country is staggering . . . yet it is not hopeless because no community is without some resources on which to build." But look around at your communities. You will find people complaining about juvenile delinquency, teen-age alcoholism, dope addiction, youthful sexual deviations and the need to do something for such kids and do it fast. Then they place obstacles in the way of those who are trying to put such children back into society healthy and whole before they become menaces. These people build with one hand and destroy with the other. By their words and actions, they let these children know that they do not count after all, that they are too sick to be bothered with, and that they should go some other place. What other place?

Montanari firmly believes that "it doesn't have to be the end of the road just because a child is severely disturbed. Such children must be loved before they are understood, and must be taught to live before they are taught to learn."

An ordinary classroom becomes disrupted by the chaos of the group, but a Montanari classroom becomes disrupted by the chaos of the individual: John snaps his pencils to splinters instead of using them to work his arithmetic; Mary reads the same sentence in her reader over and over again without proceeding to the line that follows; Jack leaps to his feet without warning and begins to scream for no apparent reason; Sue paints her hands and face and legs instead of the drawing paper on her desk; Doug refuses to write a word unless he can print each letter upside down.

Bizarre? Shocking? Sensational? Yes, but typical.

Wherever you find Montanari, you find him surrounded by such children. Complaining ("I had a bad dream last night, Monty") . . . demanding ("You promised to play ball with me, Monty") . . . entreating ("Why don't nobody ever visit me, Monty?") . . . protesting ("He hit me first, Monty") . . . embracing him ("I love you, Monty!"). As the children clamber over him, Montanari remarks with an embarrassed, sheepish grin, "They sure can wear you out, can't they?" But, clearly, he thrives on such attention.

This is Monty—sentimentalist, idealist, maverick. Against odds that would have demolished a lesser man, he has returned to society more than a thousand intensely disturbed youngsters. With rare insight, he strives to touch the minds of such troubled children in order to share with them the private demons that drive them to unhealthy emotional excess.

Perhaps in the man, as well as in the child, there lurks a demon—driving the one to emotional illness and the other to heal the illness. Perhaps, to meet the challenge imposed by such severely disturbed children, Monty, too, must keep a demon in his view.